Pelican Books

Introducing Music

Some acquaintance with the grammar and vocabulary of music – enough to understand the language without speaking it – greatly broadens the pleasure of hearing it.

Introducing Music makes the attempt to convey the elements of the art to music-lovers with no technical knowledge. Setting out from the relatively open ground of tones, pitches, timbres, sharps, flats, bars and keys, Ottó Károlyi is able to conduct the reader out into the more exciting territory of dominant sevenths and symphonic structure. His text is clearly signposted by musical examples and illustrations of instruments described, and no intelligent reader should have any difficulty in following the path. On arrival at the end, in place of being confused by the technicalities of a programme note, he should be within reach of following the music in a score.

'Here is one of those rare things – an instruction book that seems to succeed completely in what it sets out to do. . . . The author develops the reader's knowledge of the language and sense of music to the stage where he can both follow, though not necessarily read from scratch, a full score, and even make sense of some of the exceedingly complex programme-notes' – *Recorder*

'He has presented the grammar of music with great clarity' – *The Times Educational Supplement*

'A great deal of information is packed into the 174 pages' – *Music in Education*

'The book is well organized in the way one subject leads progressively to the next, terms are crisply defined and explanations are lucid' – *The Times Literary Supplement*

Ottó Károlyi

Introducing Music

Penguin Books

Penguin Books Ltd., Harmondsworth, Middlesex, England
Penguin Books Inc., 7110 Ambassador Road, Baltimore, Maryland 21207, U.S.A.
Penguin Books Australia Ltd, Ringwood, Victoria, Australia
Penguin Books Canada Ltd, 41 Steelcase Road West,
Markham, Ontario, Canada
Penguin Books (N.Z.) Ltd, 182-190 Wairau Road, Auckland 10,
New Zealand

First published 1965
Reprinted 1967, 1969, 1970, 1971, 1973, 1974 (twice)

Copyright © Ottó Károlyi, 1965

Made and printed by lithography in Great Britain by
Lowe & Brydone (Printers) Ltd, Thetford, Norfolk

Set in Monotype Times

Musical illustrations drawn by Jon Bromley Barkwith
Illustrated and designed by Bruce Robertson

To my mother
and all who have helped me to study music

Contents

List of Part-Title Illustrations

Preface

Music is both an art and a science. Therefore it must be both emotionally appreciated and intellectually understood – and as with any art or any science there are no short cuts to proficiency or knowledge. The music-lover who enjoys listening to music but does not understand its language is like the tourist who goes abroad for his holiday, enjoys the landscape, the gesticulations of the natives, and the sound of their voices, but can't understand a word of what they say. He *feels*, but he can't understand.

This book provides the tools for a basic understanding of music. Even if you read it conscientiously it will not make you a musician. Nor will it teach you how to *write* music. As with any language, it takes many years of work to achieve even grammatical fluency. What it will try to do is to introduce to you the material of music and its general laws as applied by great composers. It will also give you some of the background necessary to understand what is going on technically when you are listening to music. You will, perhaps, be in the same position as the tourist who has mastered the language up to a point and when he gets to the country of his choice can at least decipher the local newspaper, understand a little of what is going on around him, has some idea of the country's topography and social structure, and can speak to the natives without becoming inarticulate.

There is one thing which would be a great help: a keyboard instrument (piano, harmonium, harpsichord, accordion), or even a children's xylophone or glockenspiel. Music, being the art of sound, has to be intelligently heard. Try to play over all the examples, even if only with one finger. Finally, to quote Schumann, 'Don't be afraid of the words "theory", "thorough-bass", "counter-point", etc.; they will meet you half-way if you do the same.'

O.K.

Guido monochus   Theodal dulo eps

Γ A B C D E F G a b c d e f g d

Part One

Sounds and Symbols

All things began in order, so shall they end, and so shall they begin again; according to the ordainer of order and mystical mathematics of the city of heaven.
– Sir Thomas Browne

Sound: the Material of Music

In the beginning, we may suppose, there was silence. There was silence because there was no motion, and therefore no vibration could move the air – a phenomenon of fundamental importance in producing sound. The creation of the world, however it came about, must have been accompanied by motion – and therefore sound. Perhaps this is why music has such magical importance for primitive peoples, often signifying life and death. Right through its history, in all its varying forms, music has kept its transcendental significance.

Sound can only be produced by a kind of motion. The motion (or *vibration*) arising from a vibrating body, for example a string, or the skin of a drum, generates waves of compression which travel through the air to our ear. The *speed* at which the sound travels from the vibratory body to the ear is about 1,100 feet per second. This speed naturally changes according to the condition of the atmosphere. As well as air, there are other media capable of transmitting sound, as for example water, wood, etc., but this book deals mainly with 'musical' sound and its artistic use, so our medium is air.

If the vibration is regular, the resulting sound is 'musical' and represents a note* of a definite pitch; if it is irregular the result is noise. This phenomenon can be simply illustrated by the 'graphic' method. A needle is soldered to one prong of a tuning-fork and is placed vertically over a blackened glass so as to lightly touch it. Then the tuning-fork is made to vibrate and the glass is slowly moved forward. The result is that as the tuning-fork vibrates the needle scratches a *regular* set of curves.

Every sound has three characteristic properties. Let us take an everyday example. When walking along the street we hear several sounds at the same time; cars, motorbikes, aeroplanes, radios, people walking and talking, simultaneously produce sounds of higher and lower, louder and softer degrees. With our ear we automatically distinguish between the highness of a child's voice and the lowness of a man's, the loudness of a passing plane and the hum of traffic, and we know whether the tune coming from somebody's radio is played on a trumpet or a violin. In doing this, we are unconsciously selecting the three characteristics of a sound: *pitch*, *volume*, and *quality*.

Pitch

Perception of pitch means the ability to distinguish between the highness and the lowness of a musical sound. That its pitch is high or low depends on the *frequency* (number of vibrations per second) of the vibrating body. The higher the frequency of a sound, the higher is its pitch, the lower the frequency, the lower its pitch. Physicists demonstrate this by the following experiment. A piece of metal is fixed so that it makes contact with a cog-wheel, which is then turned, thus generating vibrations in the air. If the wheel has, for example, 128 teeth, and using an adjustable motor we make it turn twice per second, we get a sound of 256 vibrations, or cycles, per second (c/s). If we make it turn once per second we get a sound of 128 vibrations, which is lower than the former, and so on.

The downward threshold of our hearing is about 16–20 vibrations per second, the upward threshold about 20,000 vibrations per second. The limit of the normal range of musical sound is best demonstrated by the fact that a

* See Appendix Four, p. 167.

mixed choir produces sound between the frequencies 64 and 1,500, and a large concert piano (with a longer keyboard than the domestic variety) ranges from about 20 c/s to 4,176 c/s.

Volume

We have seen that the pitch of a note depends entirely on the *frequency* of its vibration. The *volume* of a note depends on the *amplitude* of the vibration. More (or less) intensive vibration produces louder (or softer) sounds.

loud

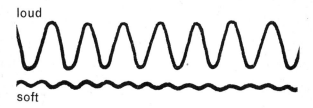

soft

Fig. 1

Quality

Quality (or in French, *timbre*) defines the difference in tone colour between a note played on different instruments or sung by different voices. Thus the 'colour' of a note enables us to distinguish between various instruments playing the same tune. No one will find it difficult to distinguish between the tone of a trumpet and a violin. But why? Here we come to one of the most fascinating of acoustic phenomena, the *overtones*. The characteristic frequency of a note is only the *fundamental* of a series of other notes which are simultaneously present over the basic one. These notes are called overtones (or partials, or harmonics). The reason why the overtones are not distinctly audible is that their intensity is less than that of the fundamental. But they are important because they determine the *quality* of a note, and they also give brilliance to the tone. What makes us able to distinguish between the quality of, say, an oboe and a horn, is the varying intensity of the overtones over the actual notes which they play.

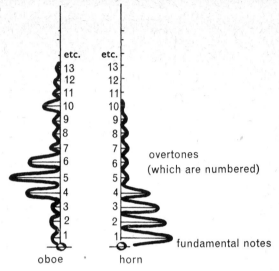

Fig. 2 (See also Fig. 85)

You can imagine what a complex wave pattern a full orchestra produces.

Before leaving the field of pure physics there are a few more points which are worth mentioning, as they are bound to crop up frequently in the listener's experience.

Standard Pitch

When we go to a concert-hall, before the concert begins we notice that at a given moment the musicians of the orchestra or ensemble adjust their instruments to a note played by the principal oboe or first violinist. They are tuning their instruments to a note which has (or should have) 440 vibrations per second.* This standard pitch was accepted by most of the Western nations at an international conference in 1939.

Intonation

Good intonation, that is, being in tune (pitching the notes accurately), has of course capital importance for the

* For the sake of mathematical simplicity, the frequencies given for the keyboard notes on the back cover assume the pitch of a′ to be 431 c/s.

musician (not to say his listeners). But what happens acoustically when we notice uneasily that something is wrong during a performance, that someone is playing too high or too low? We commonly say that the player is out of tune. What actually happens is this: if two notes have the same frequency, for example 440, we know that they have the same pitch, and so they are in unison. But if one of these is played slightly out of tune and has only 435 c/s, the result is that the former note will produce shorter waves than the latter, and these waves inevitably collide with each other, producing a pulsating effect, the number of beats produced per second being the difference between the two frequencies. In our example this would mean five beats per second. It is interesting to note that after a certain number of beats (about 30 per second) the disturbing effect diminishes.

Resonance

Some of us may have noticed that singing or whistling at a certain pitch can cause some near-by object, say, a tumbler, to resound sympathetically. This illustrates the principle of resonance: when two vibrating sources are at the same pitch, and one is set into vibration, the untouched one will take the vibration sympathetically from the other. Thus when we sing it is not our vocal cords alone which produce sound, but the sympathetic vibrations set up in the cavities of our head. The same thing happens with man-made instruments: it is the belly of the violin which actually produces the tone, by vibrating sympathetically with the bowed string. This acoustic phenomenon is very useful in reinforcing the tone of both bowed and plucked string instruments. (The viola d'amore, with its 'sympathetic' strings placed under the bowed strings, is one example of this.)

Acoustics of Auditoriums

There is another factor which very much determines, or rather modifies, the tone quality of instruments and voices. This is whether an auditorium is 'good' or 'bad' for sound, which means whether or not it possesses balanced resonance. This was instinctively felt by many composers and performers of the past, notably Bach, who, we are told, used to clap his hands and count until the sound was absorbed in order to achieve an approximate idea of the acoustics of a building where he had to play. But not till the late nineteenth century was a scientific explanation found for this phenomenon. Now we know that whether or not an auditorium is good for sound depends on the length of its 'reverberation period' (which means the length of time a sound takes to die away). Experiments have shown that the most convenient reverberation period for speech and music is between about 1 and $2\frac{1}{2}$ seconds. The acoustics of a hall can be modified by various devices, such as putting up or taking away hangings which absorb the sound.

Musical Notation

Music as well as language was long cultivated by aural transmission from generation to generation (just as folk music is still handed on today) before any kind of systematic method of writing it down was invented. But in higher civilizations the desire to record laws (scientific and non-scientific), poetry, and other permanent statements, inevitably gave rise to the problem of how to write down music. The task was to find a symbolic system which could define both the pitch and the rhythm of a melody. The roots of our European musical notation lie in the shorthand symbols which were used to note down Greek and Oriental speech recitation, the so-called *ekphonetic* notation. During the fifth to seventh centuries A.D. a system developed from these signs which vaguely indicated the outline of melodic movement; its symbols were known as *neumes*. Musical notation of this period was a kind of *aide-mémoire*. It did not define the exact pitch; it only gave an approximate idea of the melody in order to help the singer when his memory was in need of a jog – like a knot tied in a handkerchief. Then the staff first appeared in about the ninth century A.D. To begin with this was simply a single coloured horizontal line. Later, one more coloured line was added, and in his *Regulae de ignotu cantu* Guido d'Arezzo (*c.* 995–1050) suggested the use of three and four lines. The latter was accepted and preserved as the traditional staff of Gregorian chant notation, and for this purpose is still in use.

(A staff, or stave, is the horizontal line, or set of lines, used to define the pitch of a note.)

Fig. 3

From the thirteenth century onwards there took place remarkable innovations in melody, harmony, and rhythm, which led some ingenious musicians and theorists, notably Philippe de Vitry (1290–1361), who is among the many 'fathers' of musical notation, to extend the field of musical theory. Vitry's treatise *Ars Nova* explained the principles of the new art as opposed to the old (*Ars Antiqua*). The new system of notation he devised is in some respects similar to our own at the present time. However, although the five-line staff which is now used appeared as early as the eleventh century, not till the seventeenth century was there general agreement on its use. Many composers thought it necessary to use more than five lines: Frescobaldi and Sweelinck, for instance, used eight- and six-line staves.

We shall now examine the general principles of our present musical notation.

Notation of Pitch

The pitch of sounds is indicated by the first seven letters of the alphabet. For historical reasons the musical alphabet starts from C and not from A, and it is arranged thus: C D E F G A B, closing again with C, so producing an *interval* from C to C of eight *notes*. These eight notes are represented by the white keys on the piano (see back cover).

Here we run up against a linguistic difficulty which we must sort out before going any further. In English usage the word 'note' applied to music can mean three things: (1) a single sound; (2) the *written* symbol of a musical sound; (3) (more rarely) a key on the piano or other instrument. To avoid confusion I shall for the present use the word 'key' for the third meaning, and shall try to make it clear by context which of the meanings (1) and (2) I intend for 'note'. In this and the following paragraphs I am using the word 'note' in sense (1).

The interval of eight notes from C to C is called an *octave*. (An interval is simply the distance, or difference in pitch, between two notes: thus an interval of five notes is a fifth, of four notes, a fourth, and so on. Both first and last notes are counted.) The ratio between the frequencies of the two Cs (see the acoustical discussion on p. 12) is 1 : 2. Therefore if the frequency of the chosen C is 256 (this is in fact middle C on the piano) the frequency of the next C upwards will be 512, and downwards, 128.

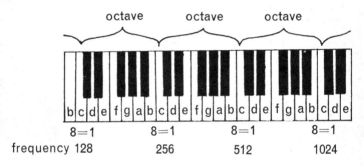

Fig. 4

If you play together two Cs an octave apart on the piano, your ear will immediately confirm that there is a special and peculiar relationship between them: they sound 'the same but different'. The mathematical relationship of their frequencies will explain why.

On the same principle, we can count an octave from any of the letters. Thus D to D, E to E, etc., are in the same ratio as C to C. Looking at the white keys of a piano, it is easy to recognize the underlying principle of how musical sounds are divided into logical proportions. Most piano keyboards are divided into seven octaves. Starting from the lowest octave their names are: Contra, Great, Small, One-line, Two-line, etc. The usual abbreviations (indicating for example the exact position of C) are: C_1, C, c, c', c'', c''', c''''.

But such letters stand only as milestones in a vast

territory. As we have seen, the most convenient method of orientation so far evolved for defining the pitch of a note is the use of groups of five horizontal lines (the staff). One group is used for the notes from c′ (middle C) upwards, and another similar group for the notes from c′ downwards, placed parallel under the first, but at a short distance from it.

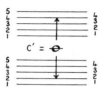

Fig. 5

Both the lines themselves and the spaces between them are used as 'positions' for the notes, but even so it is obvious that two groups of five lines and four spaces are not enough for all the notes. To get over this difficulty short *ledger lines* are added when necessary to the main lines.

Fig. 6

These lines are the shortened remainders from the time when more than five lines were used in a group.

In order to find one's way over this musical map with ease it is necessary to have a kind of compass bearing, to which one can orientate oneself: in musical terms, to know what are the exact pitches represented by the letters. This purpose is served in music by the *clefs*. There are three kinds of clefs – the G clef, the F clef, and the C clef, of which the G and F clefs are the most commonly used. They are usually known as the Treble and Bass clefs.

Fig. 7 = G clef; = F clef; = C clef

From their names we can guess that each represents a certain letter of the musical alphabet. The centre of the G clef sign goes on the second line of the staff, showing that the second line is the place for g'.

Fig. 8

It is simple to work out the relation of the other notes to g'.

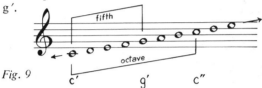

Fig. 9

Note that c' is on the first ledger line, and that g' is a fifth away from it. We see therefore that once a clef is given, each line and space represents a constant *letter*, and thus pitch.

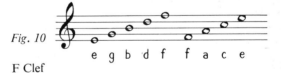

Fig. 10

F Clef

The problem of locating the lower octaves was solved in a similar way. But to distinguish it from the G clef a new clef, the F clef, was used. Its head, and also the two dots (above and below the fourth line) indicate that in the F clef the fourth line of the staff is the place for F. The place of the other notes can be worked out in relation to F, in the same way as with the G clef.

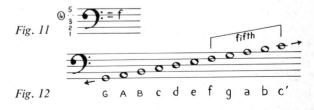

Fig. 11

Fig. 12

The reappearance of c′ on the first ledger line going upwards shows how these octaves join each other, thus achieving an undisturbed continuity.

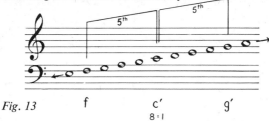

Fig. 13   f   c′   g′

8 = 1

Often in violin, piano, and other music, it is necessary to write very high or very low notes. This involves the use of many ledger lines, which is tiring for the eyes. The solution of this problem is to write the notes an octave lower (or higher), putting the sign *8va* over or under them, thus indicating that they should be played an octave higher or lower.

Fig. 14

In writing for piano, as well as for other instruments or voices where parts belong together, unity is stressed by using a *brace*.

C Clefs

From about the middle of the eighteenth century the use of the C clefs has been slowly diminishing, but two of them are still frequently used in both vocal and instrumental music. Their names are the Alto and Tenor clefs. When one has understood the principle of the G and F clefs, the use of these two C clefs does not present new difficulties. The centre of the Alto clef is on the third line, and the centre of the Tenor clef is on the fourth line of the staff.

Fig. 15   Alto clef   Tenor clef

They both indicate the position of c′. Fig. 16 shows how the C clefs are related to the staff, and to the G and F clefs.

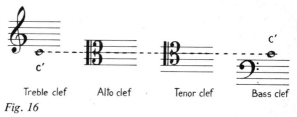

Treble clef   Alto clef   Tenor clef   Bass clef

Fig. 16

The reason for using the C clefs is that with them it is often possible to avoid the use of too many ledger lines.

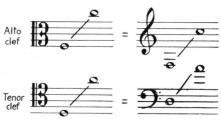

Fig. 17

The Length of Sounds

Music takes place in time, and so musicians have to organize it in terms not only of pitch but also of *duration*. They must choose whether the sounds they use shall be shorter or longer, according to the artistic purpose they wish them to serve.

We have already seen that in order to represent a sound, apart from 'naming' it alphabetically, we use a little oval sign. This is called a *note* (see p. 19). There are two kinds of written notes, white and black (not to be confused with the black and white *keys* on the piano).

Fig. 18   white note   black note

The function of notes is twofold. Besides indicating pitch, they also serve as signs for the length, or duration, of a sound. How? It is a simple matter of geometrical progression.

At the present the longest note in general use is the *semibreve*, which serves as the basic unit of length. This is divided into 2 minims, 4 crotchets, 8 quavers, 16 semiquavers, 32 demisemiquavers, and 64 hemidemisemiquavers. (Further division can theoretically be made, but the musical use of division 128 is so exceptional that it is only a curiosity. An example can be found in the second movement of Beethoven's piano sonata, Op. 81.) They are distinguished by the use of *stems* and *tails* attached to the black and white notes. Here they are:

○ = semibreve   ♩ = minim   ,   ♩ = crotchet
♪ = quaver   ♬ = semiquaver   ♬ = demisemiquaver
♬ = hemidemisemiquaver

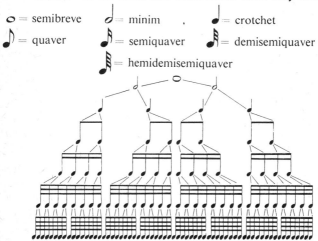

Fig. 19 shows how the sound lengths are divided.

See also Appendix Four, p. 167.

Readers may find that in some scores a longer note than the semibreve is used. This is the breve (𝄻), which as its name suggests is twice the length of the semibreve.

When several notes with tails occur together, it is usual to join up their stems thus:

Fig. 20

Here it is necessary to make a short detour in order to show how notes should be written on the staff. The main principle is to make the writing as clear as possible to read, and to group the notes in such a way that they always represent a recognizable unity. Therefore Fig. 21a is not right because it is not clear whether the note is on the third line or between the second and third lines. Fig. 21b is correct.

Fig. 21a   *Fig. 21b*

It is generally agreed that the stem of a note should be written upwards when the note is on the third line and below, and downwards when it is on the third line and above.

Fig. 22

But if several notes of smaller value have to be grouped together, the stems will be attached to each other regardless of whether some of the notes are above or below the middle lines.

Fig. 23

In the case of song, where both sounds and words appear, the general practice is to write a separate note for each new syllable.

25 Musical Notation

Dots, Ties, and Pauses

The prolonging of the time value of a note is indicated by using a dot (or dots), tie, or pause. A *dot* put after the head of a note represents exactly half the value of the note itself. Thus:

Fig. 24

In the case of two dots, the second dot adds half of the value of the first dot. Therefore a double dotted minim indicates the length of a minim, (and its half) a crotchet, (and its half) a quaver.

A tie (which is a slightly curved line ⌒) serves to attach two notes of the *same pitch*. Thus the sound of the first note will be elongated according to the time value of the attached note. For reasons of clarity, it is often preferable to use tied notes instead of a dotted note. (See for example Fig. 44 (c).)

Fig. 25

The pause sign (or *fermata*) looks like this: ⌒ and where it appears it means that the time value of the note should be prolonged. Notes with pauses are usually held for twice the normal length, but they can be longer or shorter according to musical taste. The pause often appears at the end of a composition.

Fig. 26

Rests

In speech we can sometimes make our meaning more effective by making a short pause after a word or sentence than by using more words or sentences. And in any case we need time to take breath and think before going further.

26 Rhythm

In music such silences are indicated by a sign called a *rest*. The principle of rests is simple. Every type of note has its own rest of similar time value.

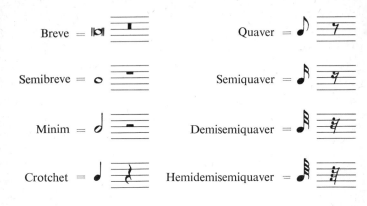

Fig. 27

Note that the semibreve rest *hangs* below the fourth line, and that the minim rest *sits* on the third line. Rests can be both dotted and marked with pauses, like notes, but never tied.

Rhythm

The observation of nature provides us with the first evidence of the presence of rhythm in the universe. The alternation of day and night, the continually rolling waves of the sea, our heart-beats, and our breathing, suggest that rhythm is something strongly connected with movement which regularly reappears in time. This pulse can be noticed even in our everyday speech, but it is with poetry, where words and syllables are more or less strictly grouped into an order, that we become specially aware of it. Here is the first line of a Shakespeare sonnet:

Farewéll! thou árt too déar for my posséssing. . . .

The accents indicate the places where the pulse has its main stresses.

27 Rhythm

In music, where rhythm has probably reached its highest conscious systematization, this regular pulse, or *beat*, appears in groups of two, three, and their compound combinations. The first beat of each group is accented. The metrical unit from one accent to the next is called a *bar*. This unit is marked out in written music by vertical lines drawn through the staff in front of each accented beat. These are the *bar-lines*. The end of a musical piece (or section within a piece) is indicated by a *double bar-line*.

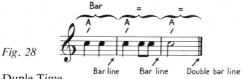

Fig. 28

Duple Time

If the beats are grouped in twos, with one strong beat alternating with one weak beat, we get bars of two beats. This is indicated by a figure written after the clef and between the fifth and third lines of the staff.

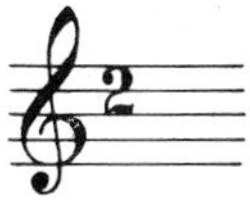

Fig. 29a

Now in order to indicate which kind of note is to serve as the basic unit of time in the bar, a second figure is written under the first. In Fig. 29b the 4 indicates a quarter-note, or crotchet.

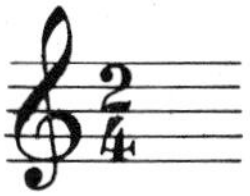

Fig. 29b

The two figures, in the form of a fraction, are the *time signature*. The following table gives the most common time signatures in duple time.

$\frac{2}{2}$ = = 2 half-notes, or minims

$\frac{2}{4}$ = = 2 quarter-notes, or crotchets

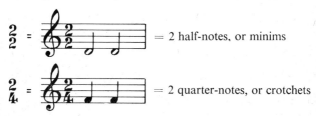

28 Rhythm

Fig. 30

Fig. 31 gives a memorable example of duple time as used by Beethoven.

Fig. 31 Beethoven: 7th Symphony, 2nd movement

Triple Time

When beats are grouped in threes, i.e. with one strong and two relatively weaker beats in a bar, we get triple time.

Fig. 32

Waltzes are of course in triple time, and through the centuries this measure has often been used for dances, the minuet for example.

Fig. 33 Haydn: Symphony No. 97 in C major

29 Rhythm

Quadruple Time

Quadruple time can be described as double duple time. In quadruple time there are two groups of two beats, with a secondary accent on the third beat.

Fig. 34

The most frequently used quadruple times and their signatures are:

Fig. 35

The sign C is often substituted for $\frac{4}{4}$, which is also called 'common time'. This C does not stand for Common, but is a relic of the period when triple time was considered as 'perfect' time because of its analogy with the Holy Trinity, and was symbolized by a circle. On the other hand quadruple time was considered 'imperfect', and was therefore symbolized by an incomplete circle.

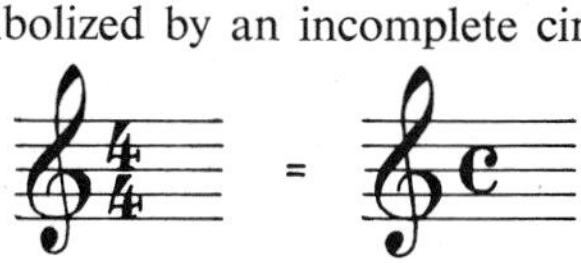

Fig. 36

The first four bars of Bach's well-known chorale 'Herzlich tut mich verlangen' give a good example of quadruple time. Note the time signature, the pauses, and also the sign showing that the passage is to be repeated.

Fig. 37

This example also illustrates the principle that if the opening bar of a piece is incomplete the last bar should supply the missing time value, thus completing the symmetry of the whole. Here the opening 'upbeat' completes the time value of the last bar.

Compound Time

The times discussed above are all so-called 'simple' times. If the 'numerator' of a simple time signature is multiplied by three, we get 'compound' time. For example, $\frac{2}{4}$ becomes $\frac{6}{4}$. This means that each half of the bar is divided into three equal parts.

Strong
Weak

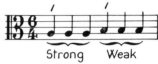

Fig. 38 (Note the (Alto) C clef!)

The most common kinds of compound duple time are:

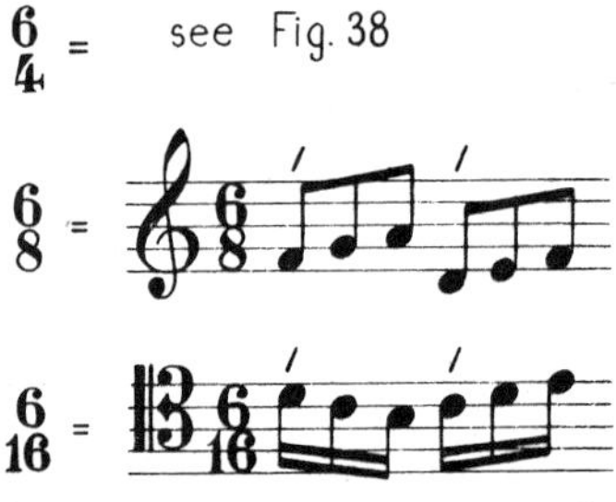

6/4 = see Fig. 38
6/8 =
6/16 =

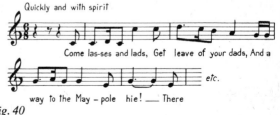

Fig. 39 (Note the (Tenor) C clef)

Fig. 40 gives a familiar example of compound duple time.

Quickly and with spirit
Come las-ses and lads, Get leave of your dads, And a
way to the May – pole hie! — There
etc.

Fig. 40

31 Rhythm

According to its accents, $\frac{12}{8}$ time can be either compound duple or compound quadruple. Fig. 41 illustrates how.

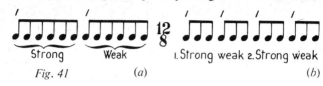

Fig. 41   *(a)*   *(b)*

The opening of Bach's St Matthew Passion is one of the noblest melodies ever written in compound quadruple time.

The most commonly used compound triple times are:

Fig. 42

Asymmetric time appears when the number of beats within a bar is five or seven. This is achieved by combining duple and triple time, for example $3+2=5$, or $2+3=5$; $4+3=7$, or $3+4=7$, or $2+3+2=7$. In each case the inner accent changes according to the combinations. These patterns instinctively appear in the folk music of central and eastern Europe and Asia, for example in Bulgaria, Hungary, and Russia. In modern music, especially in the work of Stravinsky and Bartók, plentiful examples can be found. Their usual time signatures are:

Fig. 43

32 Rhythm

Further Rhythmic Devices

Naturally no composer is content to write in perfectly
regular note-groups with a relentless beat; as in poetry,
half the game consists in *varying* the position of the stress.
The use of asymmetric time, discussed above, is one way of
introducing variety. Another much more common device
is *syncopation*, which appears in music of all kinds.
Syncopation means the deliberate changing of the normal
accent, i.e. accenting a weak instead of a strong beat.
The effect is one of tension and excitement. In European
art music syncopation first appeared at the time of the
French 'Ars nova', and from that time onwards had a
constant part in both 'serious' and 'light' musical composition. Today its Dionysiac use can be shown in all jazz
music.

The four most common methods of producing syncopation are:

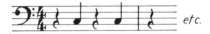

(*a*) Placing a stress on the weak beats

(*b*) Putting rests on the strong beats

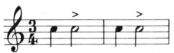

(*c*) Holding on over the strong beats

(Bartók)

(*d*) Introducing a sudden change of time signature, and
therefore of pulse

Fig. 44

Fig. 44 (*d*) also illustrates the point that as many times as the bar changes the exact time signature has to be marked.

Within a regular pulse it often happens that there are *irregular note-groups*. The most frequently used groups are called: duplet, triplet, quadruplet, quintuplet, sextuplet, and septuplet. They are always indicated by a number written above or below the group of notes, e.g.

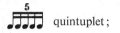 quintuplet;

and a slur is often added for greater clarity:

The way to play or think of these groups is to divide them exactly in proportion to the basic pulse.

Fig. 45

Ornaments

In music, as well as in art, an ornament is something added for decorative purposes to the main work. Its most spontaneous appearance can be found among the peasants of various nations, who often like to decorate their song by adding to it extra notes known as melismata. This they do instinctively in an improvisatory way. In art music the various decorative notes are consciously composed and clearly indicated in the notation. The most common musical ornaments are the Appoggiatura, Acciaccatura, Upper and Lower Mordents, the Turn, and the Shake or Trill. Fig. 46 shows both how they are written and how they should be executed.

Fig. 46

Tempo

Rhythm and tempo together provide the vitality, the temperament of music – one might say its nerve system. Together they determine the *character* of a composition.

Tempo is the word used to cover all the variations of *speed*, from very slow to very quick. In written music tempo markings are put over the staff, usually in Italian. The most important ones are:

35 Dynamics

Grave *very slow*	Moderato *at moderate speed*
Lento *slow*	
Largo *broadly*	Allegretto *fairly fast*
Larghetto *rather broadly*	Allegro *fast*
Adagio *in a leisurely manner*	Vivace *lively*
	Presto *very fast*
Andante *at moderate walking speed*	Prestissimo *as fast as possible*

The mark *alla breve*, also indicated by the time signature ₵, is simply another way of writing $\frac{2}{2}$.

There are many other words and phrases which are used to describe tempi more specifically. Of these, only some of the more common can be quoted here: e.g. *giusto*, strict; *assai*, and *molto*, very; *con moto*, with movement; *sostenuto*, sustained; *ma non troppo*, but not too much; *con fuoco*, with fire.

Many composers since Beethoven also give metronome marks to indicate exact tempi, and some are even content with a metronome mark alone. (A metronome is a mechanical instrument which measures the number of beats per minute at any given speed.) Stravinsky, for example, calls the first movement of his *Symphony in Three Movements* simply ♩ = 160 (i.e. 160 crotchets to the minute).

A change of tempo is also marked in Italian, as for example *più allegro*, faster; *meno mosso*, slower; *accelerando*, *stringendo*, getting gradually faster; *rallentando*, getting gradually slower; *ritenuto*, holding back; *rubato*, in flexible tempo. The indication of returning to the original tempo of the piece is *tempo primo* (= *tempo I* = *a tempo*).

Dynamics

We have already seen that volume of sound depends on amplitude of vibration. It follows that the stronger is the stimulation of a vibrating body, the louder the sound, and vice versa. If we strike the keyboard of a piano, we produce louder or softer sounds according to the vigour of our strokes. Our energy is transmitted by the sensitive keyboard construction to the sound-producing strings. The range between the very soft and the very loud sounds is divided into various degrees of volume. These are represented by *dynamic marks*.

fff = molto fortissimo *extremely loud*

ff = fortissimo *very loud*

f = forte *loud*

mf = mezzo forte *fairly loud*

mp = mezzo piano *fairly soft*

p = piano *soft*

pp = pianissimo *very soft*

ppp = molto pianissimo *extremely soft*

These marks are usually written under the staff, indicating how loudly or softly the notes should be played.

Allegro con brio

pp

Fig. 47 (Beethoven)

In a musical composition, the transition from one dynamic degree to another can be either sudden or gradual. Sudden dynamic change is indicated by putting the necessary marks under the notes wherever change is required. For this purpose some dynamic marks may be combined together, e.g. *fp*, meaning loud suddenly followed by soft. The Italian word *subito* (*sub.*), 'suddenly', is also used, e.g. *p sub.*, 'suddenly soft'. The words *più* = more, and *meno* = less, are also applied to indicate change of volume. E.g. *più forte* = more loudly, *meno piano* = less softly. Gradual transition from one dynamic to another is usually indicated by a wedge-shaped mark. It is also described in words: e.g. *crescendo* (*cresc.*) ⟨⟨⟨ = getting louder; *decrescendo* or *diminuendo* (*decresc.*, *dimin.*, or *dim.*) ⟩⟩⟩ = getting softer; *morendo* or *smorzando*, dying away.

Further 'Expression' Marks

There are various other signs which indicate special

effects. The most frequently used are: which indicates *sforzando*, or *sforzato* (*sf*, *sfz*), i.e. forcing the tone, with a strong accent; indicates *staccato*, a short pinched sound, indicates *staccatissimo*; indicates *tenuto*, and means that the note has to be held on or sustained for its exact time-value, and should be slightly accentuated; these marks are placed over or under the head of each note they refer to. The slur: lies over or under two or more notes, not necessarily of the same pitch, and indicates that they should be played as a unit, smoothly. The Italian word for this is *legato*. Sometimes the manner of performance is suggested by an adverb, such as *cantabile*, singingly; *sostenuto*, sustainedly; *dolce*, gently; *giocoso*, joyfully; *maestoso*, majestically; *grazioso*, gracefully; *animato*, animatedly.

We have had a glance at what music is made of, in terms of physics, and seen how musical sounds are written down. We shall now take a closer look at the material of music and see exactly how the various notes within the octave are related to one another: what in fact are the particular characteristics of the European musical system.

Tones and Semitones

A piano keyboard has two kinds of keys, black and white. We have seen that an octave played on the white keys, for example from c′ to c″, consists of eight notes in succession, c′ d′ e′ f′ g′ a′ b′ and c″. In playing these notes we excluded the black keys. If we play the same octave again, but now include the black keys, we have to notice that some white keys are separated from each

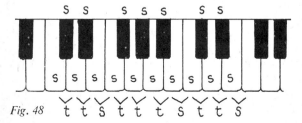

Fig. 48

other by black ones, while others are not. This shows that between neighbouring white keys there are bigger and smaller distances. The bigger ones are called *whole tones* (or simply *tones*) and the smaller ones *semitones*.

In conventional Western music, the smallest interval used is the semitone. This can be found on the piano by moving either upwards or downwards from one note to the one *immediately* adjacent to it.

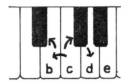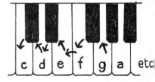

Fig. 49

Flats, Sharps, and Naturals

The signs used to indicate the raising or lowering of a note by a semitone are called *sharps* and *flats*. They look like this: ♯ (sharp), ♭ (flat), and they are placed directly *in front of* the note which they alter. Therefore C with a sharp becomes C sharp, D with a sharp, D sharp, and so on; or A with a flat becomes A flat, B with a flat, B flat, and so on.

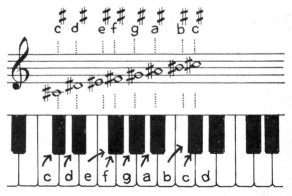

Fig. 50

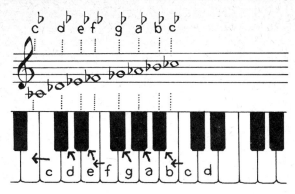

Fig. 50 (contd.)

Sometimes it is necessary to raise or lower a note by not one but two semitones (i.e. a whole tone). In this case the signs called double sharp (♯♯ or ×), and double flat (♭♭), are applied.

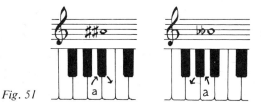

Fig. 51

In order to readjust a sharpened or flattened note to the basic pitch, for example F sharp to F, the natural sign is used (♮).

Fig. 52

Scales

We have already seen that the distance, for example, from c′ to c″ or d′ to d″ produces an interval of an octave. A scale is simply a series of notes built in progression either upwards or downwards from any note to its octave. The word 'scale' comes from the Latin 'scala', meaning 'ladder'. Therefore the comparison between the letters of the musical alphabet (or degrees of a musical scale) and the rungs of a ladder is an obvious one. There are many existing scales, for instance the *pentatonic* (five-note) scale, the Hindu *sa-grama*, the Arabian *17-tone* scale, the *whole-tone* scale, etc. The basic scale of European music is the *diatonic scale*, consisting of whole tones and semitones within an octave.

The origin of the European scale system can be traced back to the Greeks, who used to name their scales after their tribes, as for example Dorian, Phrygian, Lydian, Mixolydian. These were the principal scales, consisting of a characteristic range of whole tones and semitones in a *descending* order.

Fig. 53

Each of these scales had a subordinate companion, starting a fifth below each principal scale. Their names were the same as the principal ones, but with the addition of the Greek prefix *hypo* meaning 'under'. Therefore the subordinate scale of the Dorian was called Hypodorian, of the Lydian, Hypolydian, and so on.

Christian Church musicians, obviously influenced by the Greeks, took over their scales, but by an obscure misunderstanding they began their *modes* (as they called them) on D, E, F, and G, and, as opposed to the Greeks,

Fig. 54

took the notes in *ascending* order. Thus in the Middle Ages the Greek Dorian scale became the Phrygian Mode, the Phrygian scale became the Dorian Mode, and so on. These are the so-called *Authentic Modes*, corresponding to the Greek 'principal' scales.

The medieval equivalents to the Greek 'hypo' scales are the *Plagal Modes*, beginning a fourth below each Authentic Mode. The prefix *hypo* was adopted for them. The differentiation of a mode was marked not only by its peculiar range of whole tones and semitones, but also by its *final*, or 'home' note, which was the lowest note of an Authentic Mode. Thus the final of a melody written for example in Mixolydian Mode would be G. The final of the companion Hypomixolydian Mode would also be G.

Fig. 55

The Aeolian and Ionian modes, practically the same as our minor and major scales, were long used before they were officially accepted in the sixteenth century. Many folk songs, dances, rounds, etc. were composed in these two modes. The Church did not use them much, possibly because of their popularity and what was thought to be their secular flavour. A well-known example of early English music is the round 'Sumer is icumen in': this is in the Ionian Mode, which was disapproved of by the Church and labelled *Modus Lascivus* (the Wanton Mode).

However, the Ionian and Aeolian modes were eventually accepted and served as the basis for our modern scales. These, according to their peculiar arrangement of whole tones and semitones, are called *major* and *minor* scales. Here is perhaps the right place to warn the reader away from the common fallacy that scales come first and music only afterwards. To quote Sir Hubert Parry, 'Scales are made in the process of endeavouring to make music, and continue to be altered and modified, generation after generation, even till the art has arrived at a high degree of maturity.' In brief, creative art comes first, then follows theory.

Major Scales

If we play all the white keys on the piano from c′ to c″ we get a *major scale*. It is called major because of its characteristic range of tones and semitones.

Fig. 56

What makes a scale major is the characteristic interval between the first and the third degrees of the scale, which is called the *major third*.

Fig. 57

Each degree, or note, of a scale is indicated by a roman number, thus: I II III IV V VI VII VIII. The first note is called the *tonic* (or keynote, or sometimes, home note), and it is the most important note of the scale.

The degree next in importance is the fifth, called *dominant* because of its centre position and dominating role in both melody and harmony. The *subdominant* is the fourth degree of the scale (a fifth *below* the tonic as the dominant is a fifth *above* the tonic), and has a slightly less dominating role than the dominant.

The *leading note* is the seventh degree of the scale, and has a very important function in tonal music, that of 'leading' to the tonic, which is a semitone above it.

The *median* is the third degree of a scale, lying midway between the tonic and the dominant. The sixth degree of a scale, called *submediant*, likewise has a 'mediant' role in between the tonic and the subdominant.

The second degree of the scale, lying a whole tone above the tonic, is called the *supertonic*.

Fig. 58

43 Scales

Most people have had the experience at one time or another of singing a tune and finding in the middle that they had started it too high or too low, so that they had to begin again at a more comfortable pitch; but the change of pitch did not of course affect the melody itself. This is because the range of intervals within the melody was not altered. The same thing can be experienced with the scale. Let us now build a major scale from G instead of C: $G_t A_t B_s C_t D_t E$? .

Here we need another tone, but the interval E to F is only a semitone; therefore we must alter the pitch by a semitone: F becomes F sharp, and thus the scale can be completed.

$$G_t A_t B_s C_t D_t E_t F\sharp_s G$$

Fig. 59

Comparing the two scales of C and G, we cannot fail to see a certain similarity between them. As a matter of fact the only note which is not the same is the F. But the important thing is that they *differ in pitch*. G major starts a fifth higher than C major.

If we now try to find out which is the nearest scale to G major, we discover that it is D major, which needs only one note altering, C to C♯.

Fig. 60

This leads us to recognize an important and helpful law, that from the *dominant* of any scale a new scale can be built, which needs only one note altering from the previous scale. This note is always the leading note of the new scale.

C# Major Scale 7 Sharps

F# " " 6 "

B " " 5 "

E " " 4 "

A " " 3 "

D " " 2 "

G " " 1 "

C Major Scale No Sharps

Tonic   Dominant Leading-note

T   T   S   T   T   T   S

Fig. 61

We have already seen that the subdominant of a scale is the fourth degree upwards and the fifth degree downwards from the tonic. If we play on the piano five notes *downwards* from c′ on the white keys, we come to F, which is the subdominant of C major. Now, playing a scale from that F our ear tells us that there is only one note which needs altering: otherwise all the notes of the F major scale are similar to the C major scale. This note is the leading note of C major, which with a flattened B becomes the *subdominant* of the F major scale.

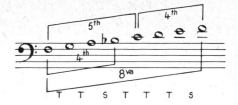

Fig. 62

The conclusion we can draw from this is that from every subdominant of a scale a new scale can be built *by flattening the leading note of the previous scale.*

C   Major Scale No Flats

F   "   "   1   "

Bb   "   "   2   "

Eb   "   "   3   "

Ab   "   "   4   "

Db   "   "   5   "

Gb   "   "   6   "

Cb   Major Scale 7 Flats

Fig. 63

The scales illustrated in Fig. 63 are those in practical use. But theoretically it is possible to build further scales, in both the dominant and subdominant directions. The result is fascinating: after reaching twelve sharps and twelve flats the two sides which started from C again 'enharmonically' in C, thus producing a complete circle, the so-called 'circle of fifths'.

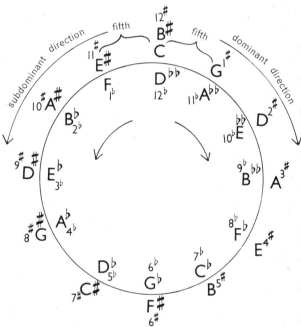

Fig. 64

Enharmonic Notes

C with a sharp is C sharp, D with a flat is D flat: on the piano these are represented by the same black key, and we therefore say that they are enharmonically equivalent. An enharmonic note is like a word with two spellings but one meaning. The diagram of the circle of fifths shows that B♯ and D♭♭ are both enharmonically equivalent to C.

Fig. 65

Tonality

Fig. 64 illustrates what we call the *key-system*. Here again we have a linguistic difficulty. The word *key* is used to mean a *note* on the piano, and this is the sense in which we have been using it so far. But it also has another very important meaning which is in no way connected with the first. It is used to define the *tonality* of a scale or piece of music, i.e. it tells us which is its *tonic* or *keynote*, towards which all the other notes gravitate. Thus we say that such and such a piece of music is *in the key of* C major or D minor, and so on, or in other words that C or D is the tonal centre of the piece. Therefore *tonal* music is music written within the *tonal* (or *key*) system, music which has a tonal (or key) centre. Note that the resemblance between the tonic and the modal final is a superficial one. The major difference between the tonal system and the modal is that tonality depends on pitch; modality is independent of pitch and depends only on certain characteristic ranges of intervals.

Key Signatures

In order to indicate in which key a composition is written, the simplest solution was not to put in the necessary accidentals (as sharps and flats are commonly called) every time, but to put them on the staff between the clef and the tempo mark. Therefore, for example in the key of D major, the required F and C sharps, indicated between the clefs and tempo marks in Fig. 66, mean that until further notice all the Fs and Cs are to be played sharp.

Fig. 66

Fig. 67 shows how the sharps and flats are indicated on the staves for all the scales from G major and F major to C♯ major and C♭ major.

Gmaj. Dmaj. Amaj. Emaj. Bmaj. F♯maj. C♯maj.

Fmaj. B♭maj. E♭maj. A♭maj. D♭maj. G♭maj. C♭maj.

Fig. 67

Minor Scales

We have seen that the characteristic interval which made a scale major was the interval between its tonic and mediant. This was called a major third, and consisted of two whole tones, e.g. C $_t$ D $_t$ E. The characteristic feature of the minor scale is that the interval between the tonic and the mediant is a whole tone and a semitone, e.g. A $_t$ B $_s$ C. This interval is called the *minor third*. Playing a scale on the white keys from A we get a row of intervals consisting of T S T T S T T. This is known as the *natural minor* scale.

Fig. 68

The interval between the seventh and the eighth degree of this scale is a whole tone, and as we know, the leading note should normally be a semitone below the tonic. Therefore in order to make it a leading note it is necessary to raise it by a semitone. In doing this we get the characteristic pattern of the *harmonic minor* scale.

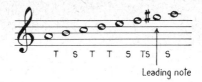

Fig. 69

Leading note

Each major scale has its companion minor scale, which has the same key signature: the submediant of a major scale is also the *tonic* of its *relative minor scale*. Or, approaching from the minor scale: the *mediant* of a minor scale is the *tonic* of its relative major scale.

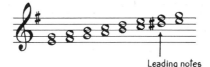

Fig. 70

Leading notes

The accidental marking the leading note of a minor scale (which you will remember had to be altered) is always stated separately, *en route*, and is never put with the key signature. (The names of minor scales are often given in small letters.)

e min. b min. f# min. c# min. g# min.   d# min.   a# min.

d min. g min. c min. f min. bb min.   eb min   ab min.

Fig. 71

This major-minor relationship shows that the law stated in connexion with the major scales (p. 43) also applies to the minor scales: a circle of fifths can also be drawn

demonstrating the relationships between the minor
scales. The only difference is that the starting note is A,
which is the relative minor of the C major scale.

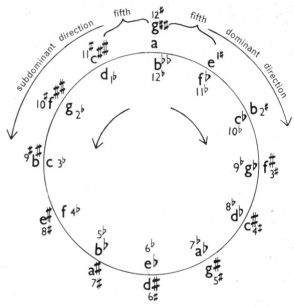

Fig. 72

Melodically, the leap of a tone and a half between the
VI and the VII of the harmonic minor scale sometimes
seems awkward. But if the sixth degree of a minor scale is
also sharpened the melodic progression becomes even.

Fig. 73

Composers in the eighteenth century and later found that
melodically it was more smooth, more satisfactory, if
going up the sixth and the seventh degrees of the scale

were sharpened, but coming down they were flattened. This kind of minor scale is called the *melodic minor scale*. Therefore all harmonic minor scales can be made 'melodic' by sharpening the sixth degree (submediant) ascending and by flattening both the seventh and sixth degrees descending.

Fig. 74

Remember that if a sharpened note is made natural this has the effect of flattening it; similarly if a flattened note is made natural this has the effect of sharpening it. The flattening of the seventh and sixth degrees when descending is by no means invariable in actual composition, as we can see for example in Bach's concerto in D minor for two violins, where in some descending passages they are not flattened.

Chromatic Scales

If we play all the notes (both white and black) from c′ to c″ we get a scale consisting of twelve semitones. This is the chromatic scale.

Fig. 75

Chromatic scales can be built from any note, both upwards and downwards, by moving from semitone to semitone. In writing chromatic scales the usual practice is to sharpen the notes going up and flatten the notes coming down.

Fig. 76

There are two more scales which deserve our attention because of their frequent appearance in the works of the late nineteenth and twentieth century composers. These are the pentatonic and the whole-tone scales.

Pentatonic Scale

The pentatonic scale (*penta*=five) consists of five notes: it can be easily produced on the piano by playing the five black keys only, beginning on F♯, thus: F♯ G♯ A♯ C♯ D♯. This scale is one of the oldest known scales, appearing as early as 2000 B.C. It is very popular among the people of various nations, and has served as the basic scale for numerous folk songs. A well-known example of a pentatonic tune is the Scottish 'Auld Lang Syne'.

Whole-tone Scale

The whole-tone scale, as its name suggests, is a scale consisting of whole tones only. Fundamentally there are only two whole-tone scales: one beginning on C and another beginning on C♯ (or its enharmonic equivalent D♭). Whatever note is the starting-point, any whole-tone scale will correspond with one of these two sequences.

Fig. 77

Though the whole-tone scale appeared in the compositions of Liszt and others, the use of this scale is very much associated with Debussy. The lack of semitones (therefore of a leading note) gives to this scale a wandering, misty quality, which served well in the musical vocabulary of the 'Impressionist' school.

Intervals

We have already met the word interval, and you will remember we defined it as the difference in pitch between two notes. We have also come across several examples of intervals such as the octave, fifth, fourth, and third, in our discussion of notation and scales. Now we shall sum up the various intervals and examine them a little more closely.

We have seen that each degree of a scale was given a roman number, thus: I II III IV V VI VII VIII. The tonic was indicated by I. The same numbers are used in naming the intervals. The first, a pseudo-interval formed by the tonic and its duplicate, is called the *unison* (unison = one sound). The term unison is also used when two or more voices or instruments play at the same pitch or an octave apart. The next interval, between I and II, is a second; between I and III, a third; between I and IV a fourth, and so on.

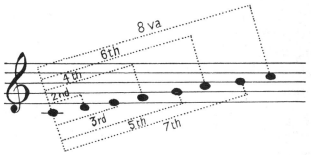

Fig. 78

This is the rough, numerical classification of intervals. But as we have seen in the case of the major and minor scales, a third can be either major or minor, according to the arrangement of its tones and semitones. This shows that apart from the numerical distinction of an interval, there are also qualitative distinctions. These are five in number: perfect, major, minor, augmented, and diminished.

Perfect intervals are the unison, fourth, fifth, and octave. The remaining intervals such as the second, third, sixth, and seventh are *major intervals*. If a major interval is reduced by a semitone we get a *minor interval*; thus C to E is a major third, but C to E♭ is a minor third; C to D is a major second, but C to D♭ is a minor second; and so on. We have seen that the ratio between the frequencies of the two notes of any octave was 1:2. The ratios between the frequencies of other intervals can also be calculated: for the fifth, 2:3; the fourth, 3:4; the major third, 4:5; the minor third, 5:6; the whole tone, 8:9, and so on. Note that the perfect intervals are characterized by the simpler fractions.

We speak about *augmentation* when a perfect or major interval is increased by a semitone. For example, C to G is a perfect fifth, but C to G♯ is an augmented fifth. Any perfect or minor interval reduced by a semitone is called *diminished*. C to G is a perfect fifth, but C to G♭ is a diminished fifth. Fig. 79 illustrates these intervals in relation to c′.

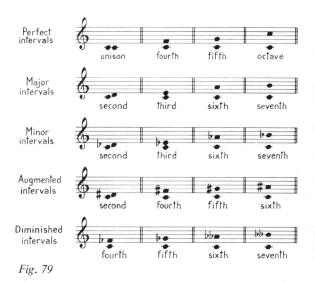

Fig. 79

The augmented fourth is also called the tritone, since it consists of three whole tones. In the Middle Ages it was called the *diabolus in musica*, because of its somewhat sinister sound.

When intervals greater than an octave are used, their names follow the numerical progression one would expect. Thus the next interval after the octave (eighth) is the ninth, which equals an octave plus a *second*.

tenth=octave plus third
eleventh=octave plus fourth
twelfth=octave plus fifth
thirteenth=octave plus sixth, etc.

These intervals greater than the octave are usually called compound intervals.

Fig. 80

Inversion of Intervals

We have seen that the subdominant of a scale is a fourth above and a fifth below the tonic. For example in C major the subdominant is F, which is a fourth above and a fifth below C. The interval between the two Fs is obviously an octave. This leads us to discover that an interval and its inversion complement each other within an octave. For example a fourth inverted becomes a fifth or a fifth inverted becomes a fourth, and a fifth and a fourth together make an octave. Therefore when inverting an interval either the lower note goes an octave higher or the higher note goes an octave lower.

Fig. 81

The tabulation of inversion is as follows:

I   unison becomes octave, octave becomes unison.
II   second becomes seventh, seventh becomes second.
III third becomes sixth, sixth becomes third.
IV fourth becomes fifth, fifth becomes fourth.
V   fifth becomes fourth, fourth becomes fifth.
VI sixth becomes third, third becomes sixth.
VII seventh becomes second, second becomes seventh.
VIII octave becomes unison, unison becomes octave.

For the sake of simplicity all the examples given in this discussion of intervals and their inversions were in C major, but the same relationships are of course to be found in any key.

We have now come to the end of our discussion of the 'rudiments' of music, which provide the basis for further theoretical study. We shall now explore some of the many ways in which composers have combined musical sounds together.

Suggestions for further reading

APEL, WILLI, *The Harvard Dictionary of Music*, Heinemann

APEL, WILLI, and DANIEL, R. T., *The Harvard Brief Dictionary of Music*, Heinemann*

BERGER, MELVIN, and CLARK, FRANK, *Science and Music from Tom-Tom to Hi-Fi*, John Murray

BUCK, P. C., *Acoustics for Musicians*, Oxford University Press

The Scope of Music, Oxford University Press

Grove's Dictionary of Music and Musicians, Macmillan

HELMHOLTZ, H. L. F., *On the Sensations of Tone*, Dover Books*

JACOBS, ARTHUR, *A New Dictionary of Music*, Penguin Books*

JEANS, SIR JAMES, *Science and Music*, Cambridge University Press*

LOWERY, H., *The Background of Music*, Hutchinson

PARRISH, CARL, *The Notation of Medieval Music*, Faber

ROBERTSON, ALEC, and STEVENS, DENIS (eds.), *The Pelican History of Music: Vol. 1, Ancient Forms to Polyphony; Vol. 2, Renaissance and Baroque; Vol. 3, Classical and Romantic*, Penguin Books*

SACHS, CURT, *Rhythm and Tempo*, Norton

SCHOLES, PERCY A., *The Oxford Companion to Music*, Oxford University Press

SEASHORE, CARL E., *Psychology of Music*, McGraw-Hill

WOOD, ALEXANDER, *The Physics of Music*, Methuen*

* Paperback edition.

Part Two

Harmony and Counterpoint

If only the whole world could feel the power of harmony . . . – Mozart

The three basic elements of music, as its historical evolution shows, are Rhythm, Melody, and Harmony. We have already seen in Part One (among other things) the significance of rhythm, its organization and notation. Now before discussing harmony, we shall briefly examine the second element: Melody, or Tune.

Melody

Melody in the physical sense is nothing else than a succession of sounds. Therefore according to this literal statement even a scale can be called a melody. But melody is of course more than that. This 'more' is the spirit which gives life and inner meaning to a succession of sounds. A scale by itself is not a melody, but a skeleton. It is the quality of inner tension which *makes* a melody.

The variability of melody is infinite, and so it is impossible to give an exact description of its properties. All the same it is possible to distinguish broadly between three kinds of melodies. The first shows a step by step progression, as for example the choral theme from Beethoven's Ninth Symphony:

Fig. 82

The next kind shows wider leaps, especially thirds, fourths, and fifths.

Fig. 83 Beethoven: Piano Sonata Op. 2 No. 1

And the third shows a combination of the first two kinds.

Fig. 84 Beethoven: Pastoral Symphony

Further examination of these melodies leads one to recognize another important feature of melody, and this is balance. In other words, in a melody tension and relaxation must be in the right proportions. An analysis of the general shape of large numbers of melodies will show that an ascending melodic line is sooner or later balanced by a descending one, and vice versa. This balance is the thing which makes a melody smooth and natural. The opening of the Pastoral Symphony quoted above is a good example of this 'naturalness'.

Harmony

Rhythm and Melody (note that melody is inseparable from rhythm – melody without rhythm becomes shapeless and meaningless) together flourished for hundreds and hundreds of years before the conscious use of harmony appeared. There is evidence that *harmony*, which is the *simultaneous combination of two or more sounds*, was used before the ninth century A.D. But it is generally agreed to count the beginning of harmonic music from the first written appearance of parallel fourths and fifths, at about the ninth century. Harmony, as opposed to melody, which is horizontally constructed, is vertical in structure.

We have seen that over a fundamental note there are other notes, called overtones, sounding simultaneously with it. The first three or four overtones can just be heard by a good ear; these are the octave, fifth, the next octave, and the following third, ranging vertically over the fundamental note. This phenomenon provides us with the first evidence of the presence of harmony in nature, and in fact it has instinctively served as the basis of our harmonic system.

Fundamental note

Fig. 85

(Each overtone is numbered)

The method of singing in unison and an octave apart is a natural one (parallel octaves automatically occur when a man and a woman sing the same tune), but the great discovery was that it was also possible to sing simultaneously at other intervals. This was discussed in a tenth-century work called *Musica Enchiriadis* in which the practical use of a melody duplicated in parallel fourths and fifths was probably first examined. These intervals happen to coincide with those of the natural range of overtones. As Fig. 85 shows, both intervals play a basic part in the overtone series.

The technique of doubling a melody at a perfect fourth or fifth was called *Organum* (nothing to do with the organ), and looked like this:

Fig. 86

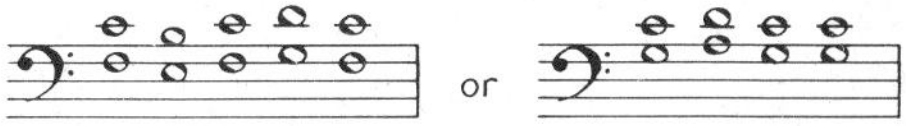

The next step was the extension of the voices into four parts by doubling both the melody, called Vox Principalis (Principal Voice) and the parallel voice, called Vox Organalis (Organ Voice).

Organ voices
Principal voices

Fig. 87

Then at about the middle of the fifteenth century the third, which is in fact the fifth partial of the overtone series, was fully accepted, and combined with the fifth to form a *triad*.

A triad is the simultaneous combination of three sounds: any note together with the third and the fifth above it.

Fifth
Third

Fig. 88

This triad is the basic element in Western harmony, and forms the cornerstone of musical theory from roughly the fifteenth century to Schoenberg. But before examining the use of harmony and counterpoint during the musical period which is the most familiar to all of us – roughly between 1700 and 1900 – one important point should be made: don't think that our major-minor tonal system is the crown of musical evolution. In art there is no progress, in the sense of *betterment*. Older or newer music than the music we know best, which is in fact no more than the product of the technique and style of a few hundred years, is as valuable as anything written between, say, Bach and Brahms. Bach's B minor Mass is not *necessarily* greater than Machaut's, or Stravinsky's; it is simply different.

After the introduction of the triad in the fifteenth century there was a rapid development of technique, which reached a splendid flowering in the sixteenth century – one of the most prolific periods of musical history. Modality was slowly abandoned and the new major-minor tonal system was established round about the end of the seventeenth century. From then until the late nineteenth this 'hierarchical' system of music seemed to be immutable. This was not so, although it is this system which, rather anachronistically, is still taught in musical academies to the virtual exclusion of others. Not without reason, however: a thorough understanding of this great period serves (or should serve) to deepen our musical appreciation of both past and present. With this aim in mind we shall now take a look at 'traditional' harmony.

Chords and their Progressions

Triads

Two or more notes sounding simultaneously are known as a *chord*. The vertical combination of *three sounds*: fundamental note, third, and fifth, gives us a chord known as a *triad* (see Fig. 88 again). The fundamental note on which a triad is built is called the *root*. We have seen that a scale was called major or minor according to the nature of its third degree. The same thing is valid in the case of a triad: the third over the root can be either major or minor. Thus we distinguish between *major* and *minor* triads. In both cases the fifth is perfect.

There are two other kinds of triads, *augmented* and *diminished*. These appear when the interval between the root and the fifth is either augmented or diminished. Both thirds of a diminished triad are minor. When the root is in the lowest part we say that the triad is in *root position*.

C major triad   C minor triad   Diminished triad   Augmented triad
in root position   in root position   in root position   in root position

Fig. 89

A triad can be built on every degree of a scale, in any key.

Fig. 90

A closer examination of each triad will show that in a major scale the triads built on the first, fourth, and fifth degrees of the scale are major; those on the second, third, and sixth are minor; and that on the seventh is a diminished triad. In a minor scale those on the first and fourth degrees are minor, those on V and VI are major, those on II and VII are diminished, and that on III is augmented.

Further examination of the triads also shows that some of them are related to each other by virtue of sharing one or two notes. For example the tonic triad shares two notes with the triad built on the third degree (mediant) and one with the triad built on the fifth degree (dominant) of the scale. Fig. 91 gives an illustration of these relationships.

Fig. 91

But if we look at the tonic triad again together with the triad built on the second degree (supertonic) of the scale, we note that they are not in close relation to each other, since they do not share any note: they are simply neighbours.

Fig. 92

65 Chords and their Progressions

We conclude therefore that between triads there are two kinds of relationships: (1) *Relation by sharing the third and/or fifth*, and (2) *Relations between neighbours who share nothing*. These relationships play an important part in chord progression.

Progression of Chords

The study of chordal progression is conventionally based on four voices: bass, tenor, alto and soprano. The reason for this is that with less than four voices one cannot always clearly illustrate all the harmonic possibilities, and more than four are too complicated to grasp at an early stage. In any case, even the most complex chords can be reduced to four parts. The names of the voices show that they correspond with the compass of human voices. These are in fact the four basic categories of the human voice, ranging between

The compasses of the voices are:

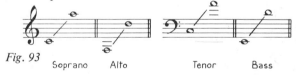

Fig. 93   Soprano   Alto   Tenor   Bass

Obviously in order to write a triad in four parts one has to add another note to the original three. This is achieved quite simply by *doubling* one note of the triad. The note which is usually doubled is the root or the fifth. The doubling of the third, especially in a major triad, is avoided when possible because it tends to weaken the function of the root. The doubling of the leading note (the seventh degree of the scale) is strictly forbidden according to the academic rules. The explanation of this is simple. The leading note is bound to lead (to *resolve*) to the tonic, and so if it is doubled a parallel octave motion is bound to appear. This, though one of the earliest forms of harmony, was during the classical period among the few 'forbidden' progressions, a convention which was only partly respected by composers but enforced by the textbooks.

The voices are arranged on the staves in such a way that the bass and tenor are written on the bass staff, the alto and soprano on the treble staff. The tails of the bass and alto point down, and the tails of the tenor and soprano point up.

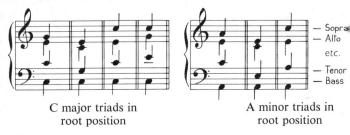

C major triads in   A minor triads in
root position   root position

Fig. 94

(Note the doubling of the root)

Fig. 94 shows a balanced spacing of the parts. An example of unbalanced spacing is given in Fig. 95.

Fig. 95

A larger space than an octave between the tenor and alto, and alto and soprano parts, is usually avoided if possible, but between the bass and tenor the use of larger intervals than the octave is common. (See Fig. 94.)

Movement from one chord to another obviously produces harmonic change. These changes of chords are generally termed 'harmonic progressions'. We all know how in speech or writing it is important that ideas and emotions should be expressed in the right words, arranged coherently, and harmoniously worked together. When this 'harmony', this logical continuity, is lacking from somebody's speech or writing we get an uneasy impression of a confused, undisciplined mind. The same is true in music.

67 Chords and their Progressions

A succession of chords haphazardly linked together will not produce a satisfying harmonic progression. As in language words must follow a logical order within a sentence, so in music chords are linked together according to 'rules' based on acoustic, aesthetic, and psychological experience. The most common chord progressions in traditional harmony can be listed as follows:

I (Tonic) can be followed by any chord.
II (Supertonic) can be followed by V, III, IV, VI, or VII.
III (Mediant) can be followed by VI, IV, II, V.
IV (Subdominant) can be followed by V, I, VI, II, VII, III.
V (Dominant) can be followed by I, VI, III, IV.
VI (Submediant) can be followed by II, V, IV, III.
VII (Seventh) can be followed by I, VI, III, V.

The voices of a chord progressing to another chord can move in three ways: (1) Two or three parts move in the same direction. This is called *Similar Motion*. (2) Two parts move in different directions. This is called *Contrary Motion*. (3) One part moves and the other does not. This is called *Oblique Motion*.

Fig. 96

So far everything would go smoothly if there were none of the taboos which make so much trouble for the student of 'academic' harmony. The most notorious of these are the *consecutive (or parallel) octaves and fifths*. For roughly five hundred years the use of parallel octaves and fifths was not generally acceptable to musical taste.

Fig. 97 Parallel octave   Unison to unison   Parallel fifth
         and fifth   or octave to octave
                            also have parallel
                            effect.

So-called 'hidden' octaves or fifths appear when two parts jump in similar motion to reach an octave or fifth. These progressions were also forbidden, although this rule was not so rigidly enforced.

Fig. 98   Hidden octave   Hidden fifth

On the other hand when the upper part moved by step the octave or fifth progression was allowable.

Fig. 99

These 'forbidden' progressions were by no means always avoided by composers; in music especially it is the exceptions which prove the rules; and the chorales of Bach, to go no further, are full of progressions which flout them. Moreover, style inevitably changes from age to age. The 'rules' of musical 'grammar' are very much like those of language. In the same way as it takes a true stylist to know just when to split an infinitive, so it takes a true musician to know when to use a parallel fifth. But from the fifteenth century to the nineteenth these rules were at least borne in mind, in order to avoid monotony in part writing.

Inversion of Chords

More harmonic and melodic variations and smoother chordal progression can be achieved by using inversion. This means that instead of having a chord in root position, i.e., with the root as the lowest note of the chord, by putting the third or the fifth as the lowest note one can change its arrangement of intervals, thus achieving more varied harmonic colours on one's musical palette. And so one speaks about a triad consisting of the root plus third plus fifth, as being *in root position when the root is the lowest part*; *in first inversion when the third is in the lowest part*; *and in second inversion when the fifth is in the lowest part*.

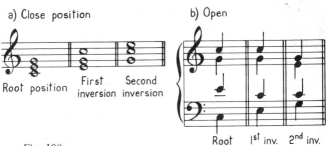

Fig. 100

There are two kinds of shorthand method used to indicate the position of a chord, *numerical* and *alphabetical*. The numerical method will be discussed under the heading *Figured Bass*. Experience shows that at the beginning it is less confusing to use the alphabetical method, which simply involves adding a small letter beside the roman number indicating degree. The shorthand indication of the chord positions looks like this:

Root position
('a' is understood by the
roman numbers alone)   I II III IV V VI VII I
First inversion   Ib IIb IIIb IVb Vb VIb VIIb Ib
Second inversion   Ic IIc IIIc IVc Vc VIc VIIc Ic

Cadences

We have seen that from the point of view of establishing tonality the most important degrees of a scale are the tonic (I), the dominant (V), and the subdominant (IV). The same is true in chord progression. In tonal music the most important chords are those built on the first, fifth, and fourth degrees of the scale. Because of this they are distinguished by being called *primary triads* (or chords); all the other chords are called *secondary*. The progressions of the primary chords (for example I IV V I) have great importance in that they indicate the end of a musical phrase. These endings are called *cadences*. If we accept the comparison of a single sound to a letter and a chord to a word, we can say that a cadence is a musical punctuation-mark. The four cadences based on the progression of the primary chords are called Perfect, Plagal, Interrupted, and Imperfect.

A *Perfect Cadence* is the progression from V to I (dominant to tonic). This progression is also called the 'full close', because of its similar function in music to that of the full stop.

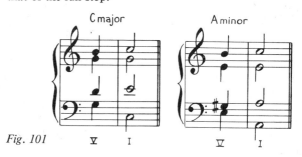

Fig. 101

A *Plagal Cadence* is the progression from IV to I (Subdominant to tonic). It is another kind of full stop. Sometimes it is also called the 'Amen' cadence, because of its frequent use for this purpose.

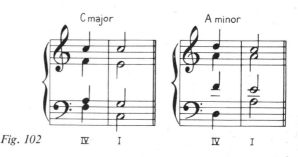

Fig. 102

An *Interrupted Cadence* is the progression from V to VI (dominant to submediant) instead of I, thus giving an inconclusive feeling which can be compared to a comma, or perhaps a dash. Obviously it cannot appear at the end of a piece, only *en route*. It is easy to recognize, since it *sounds* 'interrupted'.

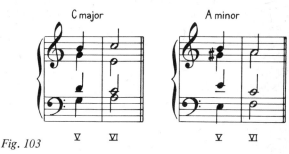

Fig. 103

An *Imperfect Cadence*, or half-close, is the progression from any chord to V. In fact it is usually preceded by II, IV, VI, or I. The imperfect cadence is something between a comma and a semi-colon, according to the context.

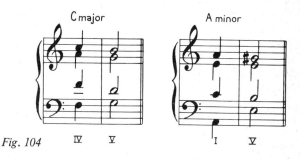

Fig. 104

When a cadence ends on a strong beat, it is called *masculine*; when it ends on a weak beat it is called *feminine* (as in poetry).

An interesting harmonic variation can be achieved by ending a piece written in a minor key with a major instead of a minor chord. This is called the Picardy third – so far nobody knows why. From about the sixteenth century to the middle of the eighteenth it was a common ending. Its effect is striking, like sudden hope after a sad event.

Fig. 105   I Ib IV   I

The four cadence formulas can be preceded by various chords, as for example II or IIb or IV, but there is one chord, the so-called *Cadential* $\frac{6}{4}$, which needs our special attention. This is nothing but the second inversion of the tonic chord (Ic). The interesting characteristic of this chord is that in spite of being a tonic chord its function is dominant. In other words, the aural satisfaction of the chord comes only when the *dominant* chord is reached.

Fig. 106   I   IIᵇ Iᶜ   V   I

This leads us to a new problem, that of consonance and dissonance.

Consonance and Dissonance

The term consonance is used to define an interval or chord which gives an agreeable, satisfying effect, as opposed to a dissonant interval or chord which gives an effect of tension. According to Helmholtz's theory, an interval is consonant when the two notes producing it share one or more overtones. The more overtones they share, the more consonant is the interval.

Fig. 107

Fig. 107 shows how the overtones of the octave are in relation to each other. In this respect consonant intervals are the octave, perfect fifth, fourth, third, and sixth. Dissonant intervals are the second, seventh, ninth, etc. The same principle is applicable in classifying a chord. A chord is consonant when it consists only of consonant intervals (e.g. octave, perfect fifth, etc.) and dissonant when it consists of one or more dissonant intervals. It is interesting to note that the first medieval theorist who considered the third to be a consonant interval was an English monk of Evesham called Walter de Odington (*c.* 1300); singing in parallel thirds – a kind of organum which was known as 'gymel' – was practised in England long before it became the custom elsewhere. The whole question of consonance and dissonance is vexed: the exact classification of intervals and chords as consonant or dissonant has fluctuated greatly during musical history. Nevertheless one fact is certain, that after a time, music without discord, as well as life without tension, becomes colourless and boring. That is what Campion felt when he wrote:

These dull notes we sing
Discords need for helps to grace them.

Dominant and Secondary Sevenths

In order to 'grace' a triad a dissonant note may be added as the fourth note of the chord. This is often the *seventh above the root*, and it is indicated by a little Arabic number 7 beside the roman number indicating degree. Fig. 108 gives an example of the most frequently used seventh chord, the *dominant seventh*.

Fig. 108

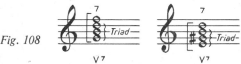

Obviously the tension produced by the seventh has to be relaxed sooner or later, or as a musician would say, 'resolved'. This means the changing of a discord to a concord. The seventh has a strong tendency to find its resolution by falling a step. And so the usual resolution of the dominant seventh chord is either to I or VI, in both of which the seventh itself resolves by falling a step. For example in C major this is the move from F to E.

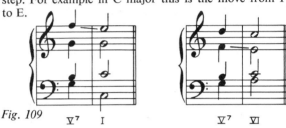

Fig. 109   V⁷   I   V⁷   VI

Note that the dominant seventh chord can be inverted, like the primary and secondary chords. The last, or third inversion (V⁷d) appears when the seventh is in the lowest part.

Fig. 110

Secondary sevenths are all the chords containing a seventh which are built on other degrees of a scale than the dominant.

All these chords can also be inverted. Thus we speak of a secondary seventh being in root, first, second, or third inversion according to whichever note is in the lowest position. The 'classical' rule for their resolution is that the seventh, as in the case of the dominant seventh, resolves by falling a step. This is achieved by moving either to a consonant chord or another dissonant chord – usually one whose root lies either a fourth above or a fifth below the root of the seventh chord.

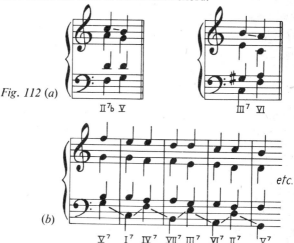

Fig. 112 (a)

II⁷b V   III⁷ VI

(b)

V⁷ I⁷ IV⁷ VII⁷ III⁷ VI⁷ II⁷ V⁷   *etc.*

Unessential or Decorative Notes

At first the word 'unessential' sounds odd, but it serves to distinguish in musical theory between a harmony note (essential) and a non-harmony note (unessential). Non-harmony or unessential notes have great importance in forming melody, and as we shall see, in harmony also, by creating dissonance. The most common 'unessential' notes are: the Passing note, Auxiliary note, Anticipation, Suspension, and Appoggiatura.

A *passing note* appears between two harmony notes a third or a second apart, and its function is to join them melodically. Passing notes usually occur on the weak beat of the bar. They can move alone, in parallel thirds, or sixths, and also chromatically.

I	Ib	IIb	II	I ——	I —	IV V⁷	I
Passing note		3ʳᵈ apart	6ᵗʰ apart			Chromatic	

Fig. 113

Auxiliary notes are like embroidery in music. There are two kinds, upper and lower auxiliary notes, and they appear decoratively between the unchanged harmony notes. Auxiliary notes, like passing notes, can move in parallel thirds and sixths, and also chromatically.

I   Ib   VI

Fig. 114   Upper and lower auxiliary note

Anticipation, as its name suggests, is the device of using a note which is sounded just before its expected time and place, and is usually shorter in time value than the note which it anticipates. It is commonly used at a cadence.

Fig. 115   I   Ib   Ic   V⁷   I

Suspension is just the opposite of anticipation; here a note arrives slightly late, or in other words its progression is delayed. With the suspension even more than with the passing, auxiliary, and anticipating notes, dissonance emerges, which has served various composers of both past and present as a means of expressing emotion. Note the characteristic tie which delays the note while the chord changes.

Fig. 116

          I   V

Rhythmically the 'unessential' notes discussed above were all weak, that is, they appeared on the weak beat or fraction of the bar. The characteristic of the *appoggiatura* is that it appears on the strong beat of a bar and resolves by moving a tone or a semitone to the weak beat.

Fig. 117

        I   V⁷b   I

Here is the place to return to the cadential ⁶₄. The fourth has always been an ambiguous interval. It has never been properly settled whether or not it is consonant or dissonant. Sometimes it seems to be one, sometimes the other. In fact when it is above a bass it is regarded as a discord. It is this which determines the move of the cadential ⁶₄. The fourth with the sixth over the root sounds like a double appoggiatura, which according to the classical rules has to resolve to the dominant chord. See Fig. 106 again.

'Exotic' Chords

Every chord discussed so far has its own clearly recognizable character and function, but there are quite a few other chords possessing a particular flavour which tends to stand out in a harmonization. Of these the commonest are the Ninth, Eleventh, Thirteenth, Diminished Seventh, and the Neapolitan, German, Italian, and French sixths.

Ninth, *Eleventh*, and *Thirteenth* chords often appear on the dominant (but note that there are plentiful examples of them built on other degrees of a scale such as I, II, or IV). As their name suggests, in each case a note lying a ninth, eleventh, or thirteenth from the root is added to the dominant seventh chord. In order to do this in four-part harmony the least important factor, the fifth of the chord, is omitted. And so the dominant ninth consists of the root plus the third plus the seventh plus the ninth; the dominant eleventh: root plus third plus seventh plus eleventh; the dominant thirteenth: root plus third plus seventh plus thirteenth. The ninth, eleventh, and thirteenth notes, being somewhat like appoggiaturas, are dissonant notes and are usually resolved by moving downwards. These chords, though often found in 'serious' music, have also been very much used by jazz musicians, so much that they are sometimes called the 'jazz chords'.

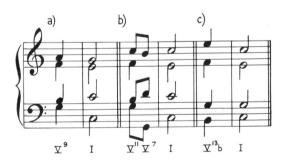

Fig. 118

We have already met the diminished triad, which can be built on the seventh degree of any scale. For example in C major the diminished triad is BDF. If we add another note to this triad, the note lying a minor third above the F, in fact A♭, we get a chord consisting of a chain of minor thirds. This is the *Diminished Seventh* chord. It is so called because in root position the interval between the root and the top note (e.g. in C major, B to A♭) is a diminished seventh. Its function is very similar to the dominant chord and its obvious resolution is either to the dominant or straight to the tonic chord. (For its peculiar properties and use see p. 82.)

Fig. 119

The *Neapolitan Sixth* chord is simply the first inversion of the supertonic triad, but with the root and the fifth of the chord lowered a semitone so as to give the chord a melancholy, languishing flavour.* It is not a discord, but because of its subdominant character its normal progression is either to the dominant or to the cadential $^6_4$. It appears as early as the time of Purcell; the origin of the name 'Neapolitan' is obscure.

Fig. 120

The *Augmented Sixth* chords are three in number and are conventionally distinguished by the names of three nations: 'French', 'German', and 'Italian'. However, it would be useless to try to make any comparison between

*In minor keys, only the root is lowered.

the nature of the chords and the nations in question. There seems to be no particular reason for the names. These chords can occur on the flattened submediant of any major scale, or the normal submediant of any minor scale, and they contain a characteristic interval, an augmented sixth. Although they are also used in inversion, their commonest appearance is in root position and their natural progression is either to the cadential $^6_4$ or straight to the dominant chord.

French sixth

C maj.   A min.

A⁶ Ⅴ I

Italian sixth

C maj.   A min.

(The third is doubled and the fifth omitted)

A⁶ Ic Ⅴ I

German sixth

C maj.   A min.

Fig. 121

Ⅳb A⁶ I Ⅴ⁷ I

A closer look at the figure will show that the French sixth consists of a bass plus major third plus augmented fourth plus augmented sixth; the Italian: bass plus major third plus augmented sixth; and the German: bass plus major third plus flattened fifth plus augmented sixth. Further analysis of each augmented sixth chord would also show that they can be thought of as chromatic alterations of the II⁷c, IVb, and IV⁷b chords.

Modulation

In art monotony is the unforgivable sin. So far we have seen that the various chords, their inversions, the use of 'unessential' notes and dissonances etc., all serve to increase variety in music. But one of the most fascinating and important technical devices of all in making variety is *modulation*. 'Modulation' means the change from one tonal centre to another. We have seen that any interval, melody, chord, etc. can be transposed* into any key, and that there is a relationship between the keys (illustrated by the circle of fifths) and also between chords. These relationships have great importance in modulation because they serve to make the change of key more smooth and natural. To take an example, the C major tonic chord can also be viewed as the dominant of F major or the subdominant of G major. Therefore the modulation from C major to G major can be easily achieved by handling the C major chord as the subdominant chord of G major, and progressing from that to the dominant and then to the tonic of G major. This kind of modulation in which one chord is common to both the initial key and the new one, thus serving as a 'pivot' between them, is called 'diatonic modulation'.

C major: Vb   I ┌Ib
G major: ┌ ⌐IVb Ic V⁷   I

Fig. 122

* Transposition means the playing or writing of a melody and/or chords *in another key* than the original.

82 Modulation

From this we conclude that the easiest, most natural way of modulating from one key to another is to modulate to closely related keys. For example, in both major and minor keys, to the relative major (or minor), dominant, and subdominant keys.

Another very common kind of modulation is when there is a sudden step from a chord in one key to a quite different chord in another key. This generally involves *chromatic* alteration. But even in this case at least one note must be common to both chords.

Fig. 123

C major: V⁷b   I
B♭ major: V⁷b   I

The third kind of modulation is also based on the 'pivot' principle, but here one or more notes of a chord are enharmonically changed to another chord of a different key. Hence its name *enharmonic modulation*. Here some of the 'exotic' chords come in very useful. The diminished seventh, the Neapolitan sixth, and the German sixth are extremely handy in modulating from one key to another unrelated, 'remote' key. For example, modulating from C major to G♭ major might seem exceptionally difficult at first sight. However, this can easily be done by using either the diminished seventh or the Neapolitan sixth as a pivot.

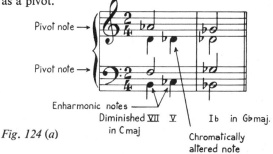

Pivot note →

Pivot note →

Enharmonic notes
Diminished VII   V   Ib   in G♭maj.
in C maj
                    Chromatically
                    altered note

Fig. 124 (a)

Fig. 124 (b)

The enharmonic use of the German sixth is extremely useful when a modulation is needed to a key either a semitone above or below the original key. For example, the modulation from C major to D♭ major and from D♭ major back to C major.

Fig. 125 (a)

Fig. 125 (b)

Modulating Sequence

A *sequence* in musical composition means the repetition of a short musical fragment at different pitches – it is in fact a kind of transposition *en route*. This can be (and often is) successfully achieved without modulation, but usually it is more effective when combined with modulation. Fig. 126 illustrates the principle of the modulating sequence.

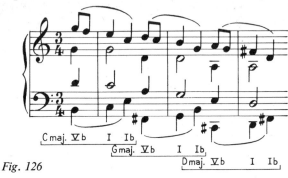

Cmaj. Ⅴb   I   Ib
  Gmaj. Ⅴb   I   Ib
    Dmaj. Ⅴb   I   Ib

Fig. 126

The repetition usually appears no more than three or four times. The reason for this is obviously aesthetic. Too many repetitions of the same musical fragment produce monotony and give the effect of a record stuck in a groove.

Figured Bass

Here we end our brief survey of the most important topics of conventional harmony. Before going further we shall take a quick look at the so-called 'thorough' or 'figured' bass. The *Thorough-bass* or *Figured bass* system was a universally accepted shorthand system of the baroque era, which served as the indication of the basic harmony for an accompaniment. The organist or harpsichordist had to 'realize' the given indication. Needless to say, this involved an absolute technical and theoretical knowledge on the part of the player. The improvisatory ability of the baroque musician can now only be compared with that of the jazz musician, who often displays outstanding technical facility. The basic principle of this method is the indication of a chord and its position by a bass note with a number corresponding with the required interval above the note. Fig. 127 gives an illustration of this ingenious system, which is still in general use, and is perhaps the soundest, and certainly the most widely applicable method of chord indication.

Fig. 127

The given bass line was often played by a viola da gamba or 'cello as well, in order to give it extra weight, while the harpsichordist played the complete chords. In this period the chamber music, concertos, Passions, and other works frequently required a 'realizer' of the figured bass, though in modern editions the chords are usually written out already for the player.

For the sake of clarity and simplicity the examples given in the discussion of harmony were either in C major or in A minor. Of course the reader is advised to make some effort to try them out in as many keys as possible. These examples served as the necessary illustration of the basic function of the chords. For their discovery in living music, analysis of the chorales of Bach, and the piano sonatas of Haydn, Mozart, and Beethoven, is suggested. Three short examples are given below.

Fig. 128 (a) Bach: Chorale – Now praise the Lord my Soul

Fig. 128 (b) Mozart: Sonata in B♭, K.281

Fig. 128 (c) Beethoven: Sonata in F minor, Op. 57

Counterpoint

Melody represents the linear dimension of music, harmony the vertical. When a melody is sung or played all by itself, as in folk music or in Gregorian chant, the linear aspect of music is predominant. This is called *monophonic* music (Greek *monos*=one, *phone*=sound or voice). When, as for instance in the case of an accompanied song, a single melody is supported by a chordal accompaniment, we get the combination of the two dimensions. This is called *homophonic* music (Greek *homos*=same). And finally, when we get the combination of more than one melodic line of definite character, the whole welded together into harmonic coherence, as for example in the organ chorale preludes of Bach, we get *polyphonic* or *contrapuntal* music. (Greek *poly*=many; counterpoint, technically synonymous with polyphony, is derived from the Latin *punctus contra punctum*=note against note.) There are other kinds of contrapuntal music than the Bach variety, when for example the harmonic aspect is not in equal balance with the melodic (e.g. in the Middle Ages) or when the problem of harmony is looked at from a different angle than that of Bach (e.g. the time of Palestrina). But in all kinds of contrapuntal music the important feature is the independent interest of the various melodic lines, in combination with each other.

The basic technical principles of contrapuntal writing can be briefly listed as follows.

(1) *Melodic interest* and independence. This can be achieved by various devices, of which the two most important are (*a*) use of the *figure*, or clearly recognizable melodic and rhythmic theme; (*b*) *imitation*, or restatement of the 'figure' in different parts and at different pitches. (Imitation satisfies a strong impulse in human nature, and in music it has particular importance.)

(2) *Rhythmic interest* of a marked independence in every part. In contrapuntal writing rhythm has such importance that the imitation of the 'figure' is often more consciously rhythmic than melodic. This is because the ear is hardly able to follow several simultaneous melodic lines, but is extremely sensitive in distinguishing rhythmic variations.

(3) *The lower part functions as a chord-basis.* Note that, in general, the more complicated is the texture of a contrapuntal piece, the simpler is its chord-basis.

Here are the first three bars from one of Bach's Three-part Inventions in F major, which illustrate all the above points.

Fig. 129   (Note that the bass figure is also imitated)

Canon

Canon is the strictest form of contrapuntal imitation. The principle is that the imitative part repeats the basic theme exactly. This technique is something like polite conversation: 'How do you do?' (first part); 'How do you do?' (second part) etc. As the leading voice goes ahead the second voice repeats what the leading voice has said. The technical term for the leading voice is *dux* (leader) and for the following voice *comes* (follower). And then if, as often happens, there is a third, fourth, or subsequent voice, each new voice, or *comes*, in turn becomes the *dux* for the voice which follows it. *Perpetual canons*, or *rounds*, are pieces in which when the end is reached the voices go back in turn to the beginning *ad libitum*: as in 'Three Blind Mice', or 'Frère Jacques'.

The entry of the *comes* can be either at the same pitch as the *dux* or at a different pitch. Thus we speak, for example, of a canon at the fifth, fourth, octave, etc. when the entry of the *comes* is a fifth, fourth, etc. from the *dux*.

There are various virtuoso technical devices in canonic writing, for example Canon by Inversion (when the *comes* inverts the melody); Crab or Retrograde Canon (when the *comes* imitates the melody, but backwards); Augmented and Diminished canons (when the part of the *comes* is written at either double or half the time values of the *dux*). At one time the singing of canons was very popular, no doubt partly because of their often equivocal texts. They were especially fashionable in England during the seventeenth and eighteenth centuries, when they were commonly known as rounds and catches. Nowadays, ironically enough, the use of canon can be found at two extremes: in highly skilled composition and in the nursery.

Fugue

Perhaps the most mature technical and (especially in the case of Bach) artistic manifestation of contrapuntal writing is the fugue (Latin *fuga*=flight). It would be vain to try to fit all the fugues ever written into a uniform pattern. Each fugue will vary in one structural detail or another from the next. That is why eminent musicologists have denied the validity of describing the fugue as a musical *form*. They prefer to speak about 'fugal procedure' or 'texture' rather than 'form', and this is why the fugue belongs here rather than to Part Three. Nevertheless, it is possible to give a general outline of its most characteristic features.

Subject

The fugue is based on a melodic 'theme' or 'subject' of marked character, which is stated alone at the beginning and which reappears at various places and pitches during the course of the composition. The *Answer* is the imitation of the subject, usually at a perfect fifth above or a perfect fourth below it, i.e., transposed into the dominant key – thus retaining close harmonic relationship with the subject. If the imitation is exact the answer is called *real*; if it has one or more intervallic alterations according to melodic or harmonic necessity, the answer is called *tonal*.

Counter-subject

After the solo statement of the subject, the answer enters; at this point the subject does not stop, but continues simultaneously with the answer though somewhat 'against' it, providing a contrary melodic line. It is now called the *counter-subject*.

Voices

Usually, but not always, fugues are written in either three or four parts, or voices. This means that there are three or four simultaneous melodic lines moving with considerable independence, but forming at the same time satisfactory harmonic progressions. When we get a subject, answer, and then again the subject, we speak of a three-part fugue; when we have subject, answer, subject, and again answer, all following each other, we speak of a four-part fugue.

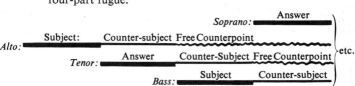

Fig. 130

Codetta

Sometimes it is melodically necessary to introduce a short *linking passage* between the 'subject' and the 'answer', or at various other points during a fugue. This is called a codetta.

Episode

The episode is a contrapuntal passage that forms a contrasting, modulatory link between the various reappearings of the main subject. Thematically it is usually, but not necessarily, derived from either the subject or the counter-subject. The use of sequences is very common in episodes.

Structure

These are the most important elements in fugal *texture*. As regards the *shape* of the whole, a fugue is conventionally divided into three sections: Exposition, Middle section, and Final section.

The *exposition* is the first part of a fugue, in which the subject appears once or more in each part (or voice). The counter-exposition may then follow as an extension of the exposition.

The *middle section* follows the exposition. Here one or more episodes are usually introduced, using various modulations, as for example to the relative, subdominant, or dominant keys. The use of long rests in one or more voices is common in this section, and serves to make the re-entering of the subject in these keys more marked.

The *final section* is generally counted from the place where the main subject returns to the tonic key, and which leads to the culmination of the whole fugue.

The final rounding-off of a fugue (or indeed of any other musical composition) is often done by adding an extra few bars to the main structure, which serve to conclude the whole piece with a flourish. This is the Coda.

All the technical devices described under the heading 'canon', and even the canon itself, can be applied within a fugue. In addition to these devices there are two more, the *stretto* and the *pedal*, which are of particular interest.

Stretto occurs when the entering of the answer takes place before the subject is completed so overlapping with it. Excitement can be increased, for example in a four-part fugue, by entering all the four voices in stretto. Stretto creates intensity, and so it is often used when building up to a climax.

The *Pedal* (or more correctly *pedal point*) is a (usually) elongated bass note over which the upper part moves ahead. It is interesting to note that this treatment, except when the pedal note fits all the harmony of the upper part (a rare occurrence), produces a series of dissonances: these were however accepted quite happily even by the academic pundits. Pedal point usually appears at the very end of a fugue (as well as in other kinds of composition) as a cadential section.

Fig. 131 serves as an illustration of a fugal exposition in E major: it comes from Bach's *Well-Tempered Clavier*, Book II.

Fig. 131

Bach's Two- and Three-part inventions, Goldberg Variations, and of course the *Well-Tempered Clavier*, Books I and II, Haydn's Sixty Canons, and Brahms's Thirteen Canons, will provide good material for the further study of contrapuntal writing.

Suggestions for further reading

COOKE, DERYCK, *The Language of Music*, Oxford University Press

HINDEMITH, PAUL, *Traditional Harmony*, Schott

KITSON, C. H., *The Evolution of Harmony*, Oxford University Press

KRENEK, ERNST, *Modal Counterpoint (in the style of the sixteenth century); Tonal Counterpoint (in the style of the eighteenth century)*, Boosey and Hawkes

MILNER, ANTHONY, *Harmony for Class Teaching*, Books 1 and 2, Novello*

MORRIS, R. O., *Figured Harmony at the Keyboard*, Parts I and II, Oxford University Press

OLROYD, GEORGE, *The Technique and Spirit of Fugue*, Oxford University Press*

PISTON, WALTER, *Counterpoint*, Norton
Harmony, Norton

RUBBRA, EDMUND, *Counterpoint*, Hutchinson

SCHOENBERG, ARNOLD, *Structural Functions of Harmony*, Williams and Norgate

THIMAN, ERIC, *Fugue for Beginners*, Oxford University Press*

WISHART, PETER, *Harmony*, Hutchinson

* Paperback edition.

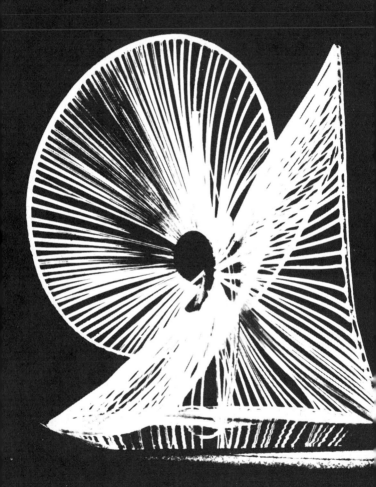

Part Three

Musical Forms

*Only when the form is quite clear to you will the spirit
become clear to you.* – Schumann

We have now become familiar with the general vocabulary of music and its symbols. We compared for example
a single sound, chord, cadence, to a letter, word, or
punctuation-mark in language. In this chapter we shall
discuss how all these materials take formal shape and are
used within the framework of a musical structure.

You may remember Goethe's description of archi-
tecture as 'frozen music'. He used the example of music
to illustrate the logical flow of a beautiful building. If we
reverse the metaphor, we can say that the bricks of music
are its *motives*, the smallest units of a musical composition.

Motive

To be intelligible, a motive has to consist of at least two
notes, and have a clearly recognizable rhythmic pattern
which gives it life. Here is a familiar one from Beethoven's
Ninth Symphony:

Fig. 132

and another from Brahms:

Fig. 133 (the opening of Symphony No. 4 in E minor)

Usually a motive consists of three, four, or more notes, as for example at the beginning of Beethoven's Fifth Symphony:

Fig. 134

It is enough to recall the continuation of the symphony for one to realize that this motive is the foundation-stone of the whole musical building. It is by means of the motive and its ingenious development (for example repetition, transposition, modification, contrapuntal use, etc.) that a composer states, and subsequently explains, his idea. But in order to explain, in music as well as in speech, it is necessary to make intelligible phrases and sentences.

Phrase

A musical *phrase* can consist of one or more motives. The end of a phrase is usually indicated by a cadence. Here lies the great importance of the cadences already discussed; they represent the necessary punctuation. Here are some examples of musical phrases:

Fig. 135 Beethoven: Piano Sonata Op. 14 No. 2

Fig. 136 Mozart: Quartet in B♭, K.589

Sentence

A common length for a musical *sentence* is eight bars. (Naturally some are longer, some shorter, but it is surprising how many are constructed within the eight-bar framework: its symmetry seems to have a peculiar fascination.) You will see how the following sentences fall naturally into two parts. The first part sounds unfinished, the second completes the statement.

Fig. 137 Beethoven: 9th Symphony, last movement

Fig. 138 Haydn: 'London' Symphony

If for the moment we take the eight-bar sentence as our norm, we can find many examples of sentences which seem to have been shortened or extended by the omission or addition of one or more bars – as in language one compresses one's thought, or puts in an extra adjective. A good example of a 'compressed' sentence is this one which begins Mozart's overture to *The Marriage of Figaro*:

Fig. 139

98 Binary Form

Sentences are lengthened, of course, by the extension of the phrases within them, and this is done by various means, such as the repetition of cadences, the use of sequences, the repetition or imitation of a bar, and so forth. The following example is from Couperin's *La Fleurie, ou La tendre Nanette.*

Fig. 140

There are naturally many other kinds of musical sentence, of varying lengths: there is no rule which can restrict a composer's inventiveness.

Binary Form

Let us now proceed from sentences to paragraphs, or in musical terms to complete structures. If we look at this Sarabande by Corelli, we immediately notice its resemblance to a question and answer in speech.

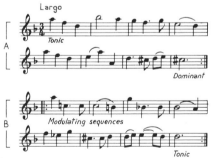

Fig. 141

It has its questioning section (A), starting in the tonic and ending in the dominant. The second answering section (B) takes its melody from the key in which A ended, modulating as it does so, and then works back

again to the tonic. This procedure is like asking somebody:

'How are you?'   and receiving the answer:
(T)   (D)
                 'I am very well, thank you.'
                           (T)

Here the 'I' of the first sentence can be regarded as the
tonic; the dominant, 'you', becomes the 'I' of the next
sentence, and the 'you' is tossed back in turn to the first
speaker, once more becoming the 'I'.

This example illustrates 'binary' form (*bi*-nary
because of its two sections). It is the simplest lay-out,
scheme, form, or plan, call it what you will, which
composers use. A musical form does not inhibit a composer: it simply provides a frame in which he can express
himself artistically. This formal discipline is like that
accepted by the poet who tries to express his thought and
emotion within the framework of, say, the sonnet.

Now let us look at an example from Bach to see how
the binary form can be extended. Here is the close of the
Allemande from the French Suite No. 6.

Fig. 142

Here we notice an extra four bars after the expected end,
giving a smooth conclusion, a little more time to settle
the piece comfortably. This is the Coda (already met with
during our discussion of the fugue).

In binary form the two sections, A and B, are often
repeated, which makes the differences between them more
pointed. When A and B are not symmetrical it is the B
section which is the longer. This is because of the richer
possibilities of modulation in working back towards the
tonic, and also because of the Coda, when there is one
(counting the Coda as part of B). Dance music of the
seventeenth and eighteenth centuries, which achieved its
most perfect expression in the suites of Bach, is mostly
in binary form.

Ternary Form

If, now that you have digested this binary formula 'A B', you are given another formula, consisting of 'A B A', you will automatically assume, and rightly, that A represents one section, B another, and that the re-appearing A must be the repetition of, or something very similar to, the first A. But if you look at Fig. 143 you will find that there is in fact a major difference between the two formulae. A B A, called 'ternary' form, differs from binary in that B is an *episode* in complete contrast to A^1 and A^2, and each of the sections is harmonically self-contained. This example is from the third movement of Beethoven's Piano Sonata in B♭, Op. 22.

Fig. 143

To summarize the general shape of the ternary form, we can call it a musical sandwich, consisting of a first section starting in the tonic and ending either in the tonic or a related key, an episode (the filling) which is contrasted with both the first and third sections by using a different key (or keys) and/or material, and a third section which is either the exact or slightly varied repetition of the first, starting and ending in the tonic. Sometimes, as in our example, a Coda is added.

Many examples of music written in this form can be found in the general musical repertoire. An early example is the Shepherd's song from Monteverdi's *Orfeo* (1607);

Bach uses it in his suites when he indicates an *alternativo* (i.e. the first of a pair of dances is repeated after the second has been played); the *da capo* aria is an obvious example; and also the Minuet+Trio+Minuet used by the composers of the classical period (Haydn, Mozart, Beethoven) as the third movement of a symphony or a sonata. And if you take a closer look at the shorter piano pieces of the Romantic era, as for example Chopin's Nocturnes and Mazurkas, and Schubert's Impromptus, you will find that many of them are ternary in form.

Forms Based on Dances

For centuries the dance had above all ritualistic and religious significance. The adoration and propitiation of the gods, prayers for fertility, good weather, and so on, were often expressed by means of dance movements and tunes, either extemporized or traditional. During the periods of the ancient Greeks and Romans the dance slowly evolved from rite to conscious art. But, sacred or secular, and whether art or not, there is something fundamentally erotic in the dance, and this did not please the Church. During the Middle Ages dance music and dancing in general were frowned on. The dance nevertheless continued among the people, and finally found its renaissance at the various European courts of the sixteenth century. Dances of often rustic origin became widely fashionable and evolved into strongly stylized instrumental pieces, to which in the end no one danced, but simply listened. This procedure finds its clear manifestation in the suite.

Suite

The suite is an instrumental composition consisting of a chain of stylized dances. It was one of the most important forms of instrumental music during the seventeenth and eighteenth centuries, and is still used, though with modifications.

The four most important types of dance which conventionally appear in a suite of the baroque era (as for example those of Bach) are the Allemande, the Courante, the Sarabande, and the Gigue.

Allemande

The Allemande is a dance of German origin in moderate quadruple ($\frac{4}{4}$) time. Its rhythmic characteristic is the upbeat (weak to strong) beginning.

Fig. 144 Bach: Solo 'Cello Suite in G major

Courante

There are two kinds of courante: Italian and French. The Italian (*corrente*, 'running') is a dance in triple time ($\frac{3}{4}$) of lively character.

Fig. 145 Handel: Suite in G minor

The French courante is in triple time ($\frac{3}{2}$ or $\frac{6}{4}$) and of a contrapuntal nature. Its peculiar characteristic is that the two metres are often interchanged, or even mixed, particularly at the cadences. The position of the accent is thus varied and the rhythm is therefore somewhat ambiguous. The whole procedure can be called *polyrhythmic*.

Fig. 146 Bach: English Suite No. 5 in E minor

Sarabande

The sarabande came from Spain, but its true origin is supposed to be Moorish or Persian. It is in a slow $\frac{3}{4}$ or $\frac{3}{2}$, with an accent on the second beat. Its character eventually became noble and dignified, but originally it was a voluptuous love dance which scandalized many prominent men of virtue.

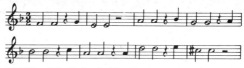

Fig. 147 Handel: Suite in D minor

Gigue

The gigue, or jig, appears as the finale of a suite. It is a fast, lively dance of English or Irish origin. Usually it is in $\frac{3}{8}$, $\frac{6}{8}$, $\frac{9}{8}$, or $\frac{12}{8}$, and its treatment is mostly imitative, often fugal.

Fig. 148 Bach: English Suite No. 5 in E minor

To the four basic constituents of the suite various other kinds of dance were often (but not always) added, as for example the Minuet (see p. 104), Gavotte ($\frac{4}{4}$), Passe-pied ($\frac{3}{8}$ or $\frac{6}{8}$), Bourrée ($\frac{4}{4}$), Musette (a pastoral dance with a kind of bagpipe drone), and the Passacaglia (see pp. 104–5). Sometimes the Allemande was preceded by an introductory movement not based on the dance, but of a somewhat improvisatory or rhapsodic nature. Such movements were the Prelude, the Fantasia, the Toccata, and others.

The various movements of the baroque suite were usually based on one key, though modulation appeared within individual movements. In later periods there were many changes, particularly in the flexible use of tonality, the adaptation of other dances than the conventional types, and finally the free linking-in of various contrasting musical forms. Examples of the suite form can be found in the Partitas of Bach, his French, English, and orchestral suites, and the suites of Handel; later examples include

Bizet's *L'Arlésienne* suite, Grieg's *Peer Gynt* suite, Stravinsky's *Firebird* suite, and Bartók's *Dance Suite*.

From the various dances of the sixteenth and seventeenth century there are three which, apart from their occasional appearance within a suite, have particular peculiarities and importance. These are the Minuet, Chaconne, and Passacaglia.

Minuet

The minuet comes from France, and was one of the officially accepted dances at the court of Louis XIV. It is in $\frac{3}{4}$ time, and originally its speed was gracefully moderate, but in the hands of Haydn and Mozart it became gradually faster. Finally, with Beethoven, its character changed so much that eventually he replaced it with the fast and lively *scherzo*.

The structure of the minuet can be either binary or ternary. The interesting peculiarity of the minuet is that it is often combined with the so-called *Trio*, which is a middle section between the minuet and its repetition. The Trio was originally played by three players only; hence its name. The outline of the Minuet and Trio form, therefore, is:

A¹   *Minuet*, written either in binary or ternary form, opening and closing in the tonic.

B   *Trio*, based on new material, which can itself be either binary or ternary in form. The key is often a new one.

A²   Repetition of A¹, with the occasional addition of a Coda.

As a complete structure the Minuet and Trio is of course ternary in form, as we have already seen.

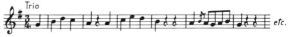

Fig. 149 Mozart: Symphony No. 40 in G minor

Chaconne and Passacaglia

The chaconne and the passacaglia were originally dance

forms in slow triple time, but they entirely lost their dance-like characteristics. The basic idea of their highly stylized treatment is continuous variation, usually over a *basso ostinato*, or 'ground bass'. *Ostinato* (Italian, 'obstinate') means the persistent repetition of a musical phrase either through the whole of a movement or episodically. The *ostinato* principle is the chief characteristic of both chaconne and passacaglia.

One of the most outstanding examples of this treatment is Bach's well-known Passacaglia in C minor for organ. In this an eight-bar-long *ostinato* theme reappears twenty times, mostly in the bass, either repeated exactly or varied very slightly.

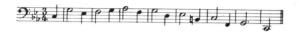

Fig. 150

The correct distinction between a chaconne and a passacaglia is still an unsolved musicological problem. But in spite of all their similarities, it is possible to say that a passacaglia is based on a marked *ostinato* melodic theme, which is usually in the bass, and that the chaconne is a continuous variation in which the 'theme' is rather a chain of chords, which serve as the basis for each variation. This is indeed a slight distinction, and it has been frequently overlooked by various composers, historians, and critics, who have in fact used the two terms interchangeably. Therefore one must not be surprised to find the last movement of Brahms's Fourth Symphony quoted once as a typical example of a passacaglia, and another time as a typical example of a chaconne.

Variations

The chaconne and the passacaglia partly belong to the category of variations, but because of their origin in the dance, and also because of their common appearance within a suite, they were discussed under the general heading 'dance'. They can now serve as a bridge to our next subject, the variation form.

106 Rondo

As one would suppose, 'variation' means the presentation of a theme several times over, but each time somewhat modified, melodically, rhythmically, or harmonically. The theme serving for variation is usually an easily grasped melody written either in binary or ternary form, but it can also be a single musical sentence. The theme may be an original composition of the composer, as for example in the case of Mozart's Variations in his A major Piano Sonata, but often it is one borrowed from another composer for a virtuoso try-out of its melodic and harmonic potentialities, as for example Beethoven's Diabelli Variations, and Brahms's Handel and Haydn Variations.

Fig. 151 gives an illustration of the Diabelli theme and also a few bars from Beethoven's first two variations on it.

Fig. 151

Rondo

The musical rondo, like the rondel or rondeau of poetry, is based on repetition. In a rondo the principal theme reappears at least three times, often more. Each time the theme and its repetition are clearly separated by a contrasting episode. The plan of a rondo therefore looks like this:

A¹ Theme in the tonic
B First episode, in another key
A² Theme in tonic
C Second episode, in another key
A³ Theme in tonic, frequently leading to a coda.

These sections are smoothly joined together when necessary by little 'linking' or 'bridging' passages. The rondo form, because of its strong resemblance to the ternary principle (A B A), is sometimes described as an extended ternary form (a double-decker sandwich).

An outstanding example of the rondo form is the Adagio from Beethoven's 'Pathétique' sonata.

Fig. 152
(This is the repetition of the theme in the Treble clef.)

The Sonata

Up till the sixteenth century instrumental music did not have major importance. Musical style was in general based on the vocal aspect of music, and instruments, when they were used at all, usually had a function subordinate to that of the voices.

The rise of instrumental music is conventionally dated from about the sixteenth century. The germ of the sonata can be traced back to this time. Originally the term 'sonata' (Italian *suonare*, to sound) meant anything which was not sung, but played on instruments. As opposed to the suite, which developed from dance music, the sonata had its roots in a vocal type of music of Franco-Flemish origin called 'chanson'. During the seventeenth and early eighteenth centuries the sonata, in contrast to the suite, usually consisted of a composition of various movements, but of a more serious character, written partly in binary and partly in ternary form. A further distinction was made between the *sonata da camera* (chamber sonata) and the *sonata da chiesa* (church sonata). However, at that time the differences between the sonata and the suite were not very sharp. Movements of dance-like character often appeared in the sonata. The Minuet and Trio movement of the Classical sonata is in fact a relic of this dualism.

From these early types of sonata, as a result of a slow evolution, in which many distinct forms were involved, and to which many composers contributed, at about the middle of the eighteenth century the sonata gained its characteristic shape, as well as supreme importance among the forms of music. The time of Haydn, Mozart, and Beethoven, the so-called classical period, bears throughout the stamp of the sonata form. It was in the hands of these composers that the sonata form reached its peak as a highly complex musical structure.

Sonata Form

From our brief historical sketch we shall now turn to take a closer look at the sonata principle.

Sonata form describes the characteristic structure of a *single movement*. The classic sonata form shows three basic divisions: exposition, development, and recapitulation.

Exposition

As in the first part of a play we are introduced to the main characters, so in the exposition of the sonata form we become acquainted with its basic thematic or subject material. This subject material, rather like the *dramatis personae* of a play, is divided into two groups, which one may characterize as masculine and feminine. The theme of the first subject (or first subject group when there is more than one thematic idea) is usually a short concise melody of marked rhythmic interest, and of 'masculine' character, in the tonic key.

Fig. 153 Beethoven: Sonata in C minor, Op. 10, no. 1

The second subject (or group) is usually of a lyrical, more 'feminine' character, in contrast to the first subject.

It can be generally said that in the second subject it is usually the melodic interest which is predominant. (Note however that sometimes the two roles are reversed and it is the lyrical subject which comes first.) But the most important contrast between the first and second subject is that the second is in a different key. This is often the dominant, or the relative major or minor.

Fig. 154 Beethoven: Sonata in C minor, Op. 10, no. 1

The transition between the two groups is made by a modulating 'bridge' passage of varying length, usually based on the thematic material of the first subject. To take our theatrical analogy further, one could call this new 'character' a friend of both husband and wife.

The exposition closes with a codetta. At that point, unless there is a complete repetition of the exposition, as sometimes happens, the development begins.

Development

In the development the given material is worked up to a climax. We here become acquainted with the whole dramatic conflict, which is expressed by various musical means such as modulation, the use of imperfect and interrupted cadences, melodic decorations, dynamic tension, etc. Again, the resemblance to the development of a play seems obvious.

Recapitulation

The recapitulation is the concluding section, in which the exposition is repeated, but with some technical and emotional modifications. The important technical modification is that the second subject is now in the tonic key. The whole leads to a coda. The conflict is over, the characters have regained their equilibrium – but, as a result of the events they have experienced, they have subtly changed.

As a complete structure the sonata form can be

described, broadly speaking, as ternary in outline (A^1 B A^2).

As a general term, 'sonata' defines an instrumental composition of various movements for one or two instruments, *in which one or more of the movements is in sonata form*. This is most frequently the first movement, and because of this sonata form is often misleadingly referred to as 'first movement form'.

The sonata as a whole usually consists of three, or more frequently four, movements. The common plan of a sonata of four movements is:

1st movement: Sonata form.

2nd movement: Ternary form (but can also be Sonata form, Rondo, Variations, etc.)

3rd movement: Minuet and Trio (or Scherzo and Trio)

4th movement: Rondo (or Sonata form, sometimes Variations).

Their usual tempo indications are based on the aesthetical principle of balanced variety, and are commonly: (1) Fast; (2) Slow; (3) Moderately fast; (4) Fast.

When more than one or two instruments are involved the name of the composition becomes Trio, Quartet, Quintet, etc. Therefore a String Quartet, for example, is really a Sonata for four stringed instruments: two violins, one viola, and one 'cello. When a full orchestra is involved we speak of a Symphony.

Sometimes such works are preceded by an Introduction. This is a musical section which, as its name indicates, serves to introduce the movement which follows it. It can be quite short, as for example the two-bar introduction to Beethoven's Eroica Symphony, or much longer, as in his Seventh.

Sonata Rondo

The sonata rondo is an interesting combination of two forms, the rondo and the sonata form. It often appears as the last movement of a sonata. The outline of the form looks like this:

Exposition
- A¹ *Rondo theme*, serving as the *first subject* in the tonic.
- B¹ *First episode*, which introduces the *second subject*, in the dominant or another key.
- A² *Rondo theme*, first subject in tonic.

Development
- C *Second, or central episode*, in which development may take place.

Recapitulation
- A³ *Rondo theme*, first subject in tonic.
- B² *Third episode*, in which the second subject re-appears, but now in the tonic (exactly as in the sonata form).
- A⁴ *Rondo theme*, leading to the Coda.

There are plentiful examples of this form in the repertoire of Haydn, Mozart, and Beethoven. A well-known example is the last movement of Beethoven's Eighth Symphony. Here is the theme:

Fig. 155

Symphony

The symphony is simply the adaptation of the sonata for full orchestra. Owing to its greater musical possibilities – especially of colour and climax – symphonic writing has an imposing place in the history of music. It is the large-scale novel of musical literature; within its instrumental range there is room for everything from the most delicate lyricism to the expression of heroic struggle. The common plan for a symphony is similar to the sonata plan given on page 110.

Concerto

The concerto is a composition for solo instrument (or instruments) and orchestra in which the two sides, so to speak, complement each other (Latin *concertare*=to fight side by side).

When a small *group* of instruments (called *principale* or *concertino*) competes with the full orchestra (called *tutti* or *ripieno*), the work is called *Concerto Grosso*. This was one of the most important types of orchestral music of the baroque period. At first it contained a larger number of movements, but with Vivaldi the succession of three movements – quick, slow, quick – was established.

The concertos of Corelli, Vivaldi, Bach, and Handel, show examples of both types. After a long pause, the concerto grosso treatment has been revived to some extent among modern composers, for instance Bartók and Hindemith, who have both written a Concerto for Orchestra.

The sólo concerto involves the display of a solo instrument with the accompaniment (which does not necessarily mean subordination) of an orchestra. Sometimes two, three, or even four solo instruments are used, in which case the name of the work is 'double concerto', 'triple concerto', 'sinfonia concertante', etc. From the Viennese classics onwards the concerto commonly contained three movements. These correspond in structure to the first, second, and fourth movements of a sonata (omitting the Minuet and Trio). As a part of the first, and sometimes also of the other two movements, the *cadenza* is inserted. This is simply an opportunity for technical showing off by the soloist while the orchestra is in silence. Its usual place is at the end of the recapitulation, beginning from a cadential $^6_4$ chord (Ic) and ending on the dominant (V), where the orchestra re-enters (*tutti*) and brings the movement to a close. Originally the soloist improvised his cadenza, which was based on the main theme of the movement. But from Beethoven onwards the cadenza is usually written by the composer.

Overture

The overture is an instrumental composition which, as

its name suggests, serves to introduce an opera, oratorio, or similar composition. In the operas of the early seventeenth century, when it appeared at all, it was no more than a kind of signal in order to compel the attention of the audience before the beginning of the work proper. From this utilitarian item evolved the two standard types of overture, 'French' and 'Italian'.

The *French overture* is associated with Lully, the Italian-born court musician of 'Le Roi Soleil'. Originally the French overture had two sections: a *slow* one written in a solemn if not pompous style, with a predominance of dotted rhythms; and a *quick* one of a somewhat lightly and freely treated contrapuntal style. Often this led to a coda-like slow passage which was eventually enlarged into a third section. Sometimes the opening slow material was repeated, or a movement of dance character was added to the two main sections. The overture to Handel's *Messiah* is a well-known example of the French type.

The *Italian overture* was introduced by the Italian Alessandro Scarlatti, a younger contemporary of Lully, who was one of the founders of the Neapolitan school of opera. This overture consisted of three sections in basically homophonic style – quick, slow, quick. At that time it was commonly called 'sinfonia', meaning an overture before an opera. During the eighteenth century the French type of overture was slowly eclipsed and the overture became a simple movement in sonata-like form, as for instance the overture to Mozart's *The Magic Flute*. With Wagner this was transformed into a freely handled thematic 'directory' which leads right into the opening scene of the opera, as in *The Mastersingers*.

The *concert overture* is an independent orchestral composition, which has no connexion with any operatic or other work. Its form is often a loose sonata form, but many other types of form are also used. Examples of concert overtures are Berlioz' *Le Carnaval Romain* and Brahms's Academic Festival Overture.

However, overtures which have a connexion with an operatic or dramatic composition are often performed as concert overtures, for example Beethoven's *Leonora* and *Coriolanus* overtures.

Vocal Forms

As opposed to the 'folk' song, whose origin is anonymous, and which crystallizes or degenerates according to the instinctive aesthetic sense of the people who hand it down aurally from generation to generation, the 'art' song is consciously written by a composer. Good or bad, it is on paper, he is fully responsible for it. To this category belong the Aria and the Lied. The two words simply mean 'song' in Italian and German. However, they are now used internationally to distinguish between two kinds of 'art' song.

Aria

The aria is a solo vocal composition built on a larger scale than a simple song would be, with an instrumental accompaniment. The choice of its form is quite free: binary form, ternary form, rondo, passacaglia, etc. can all serve as the formal structure of the aria. The *da capo* aria (Italian *da capo* = from the beginning) shows a fixed three-part structure which is achieved by the repetition of its first section after a contrasting second section. This is an obvious example of ternary form. The *da capo* indication (abbreviation D.C.) is written at the end of the aria.

Recitative

Although not a musical form in itself, the recitative has marked importance in connexion with operatic vocal style (i.e. in opera, oratorio, Passion, etc.). It indicates a somewhat speech-like vocal style based on a text of a narrative or declamatory nature. In the recitative, melody, rhythm, and phrase are subordinated to speech-like inflection. Unlike the aria, it has no definite form, its real function being that of connecting and carrying forward the development of the story, as for example the Evangelist does in Bach's St Matthew Passion. And so the recitative precedes or follows arias, choruses, etc., thus securing the continuity of the action. Musicians distinguish between two kinds of recitative, *secco* (Italian, dry) and *accompagnato* (Italian, accompanied). In the case of the *recitativo secco* the accompaniment of the singer is no more than punctuating chords (usually cadences) played on the key-board, reinforced in the bass by 'cello or viola da gamba; with the *recitativo accompagnato* the accompaniment is played by the orchestra or a smaller instrumental group.

Numerous examples of arias, *da capo* arias, and recitatives can be found in the operatic repertoire of the eighteenth century and to some extent the nineteenth. It is enough simply to mention the names of Bach, Handel, Mozart, Rossini, and Verdi, to bring familiar examples to mind. One need go no further than Handel's *Messiah* to find instances of all three forms.

Lied

The 'Lied' is primarily associated with the German Romantic period, and above all with the name of Schubert. The Lied in its general interpretation means a song based on poetry with a piano accompaniment. But the most important characteristic of the Lied is that its piano part is not merely a decorative support to the song, but an integral and equal part of it. The miraculous artistic achievement of the young Schubert is just this, that the inner meaning of the poetical text is expressed by voice and instrument in an unsurpassed unity. (See Schubert's *Death and the Maiden*, *The Erl-king*, etc.) The form of the Lied can be anything which suits best the musical expression of the text.

A *song cycle* is a set of songs (*Lieder*) which are connected in thought, thus forming an artistic unity. Examples of this are Schubert's *Die schöne Müllerin*, and Schumann's *Dichterliebe*.

Separate discussion of the mass, cantata, opera, oratorio, and so forth, is here omitted, partly for reasons of space, but also because they are not really distinct musical forms, but rather a welding-together of many forms, all of which we have already dealt with in this chapter. In the opera, for example, we have, or can have, a gigantic amalgam of all the musical forms which exist, with the inclusion of drama, poetry, prose, decorative art, and dance for good measure.

Programme Music

This term does not imply a particular form, but it is a

general description for music which is under the influence of a non-musical subject, say a picture or a story. Here the aim of the composer is to illustrate as far as possible in musical terms this extra-musical idea. Examples of programme music are Berlioz' *Symphonie Fantastique*, Richard Strauss's *Till Eulenspiegel*, and Debussy's *Prélude à l'après-midi d'un faune*.

The *symphonic poem* belongs to the category of programme music. The term describes a programmatic orchestral composition which usually contains one movement in a freely adapted sonata form.

We have now discussed the most important kinds of musical form which are likely to be encountered by the listener. Obviously this introduction could not cover all the existing types of composition: these can be studied in the various books suggested on p. 117.

Suggestions for further reading

CROCKER, RICHARD, L., *A History of Musical Style*, McGraw-Hill

DAVIE, CEDRIC THORPE, *Musical Structure and Design*, Dobson

DENT, EDWARD, J., *Opera*, Penguin Books*

GROUT, D. J., *A Short History of Opera*, Oxford University Press

HARMAN, ALEC, and MELLERS, WILFRID, *Man and His Music*, Barrie and Rockliff

HILL, RALPH (ed.), *The Concerto*, Penguin Books*

HOPKINS, ANTONY, *Talking About Symphonies**; *Talking About Sonatas* and *Talking About Concertos*, Heinemann

JACOBS, ARTHUR (ed.), *Choral Music; A Short History of Western Music*, Penguin Books*

LANG, P. H., *Music in Western Civilization*, Dent

LEICHTENTRITT, HUGO, *Musical Form*, Harvard University Press

MATTHEWS, DENIS (ed.), *Keyboard Music*, Penguin Books*

RÉTI, RUDOLPH. *The Thematic Process in Music*, Macmillan (New York)

ROBERTSON, ALEC (ed.), *Chamber Music*, Penguin Books*

SIMPSON, ROBERT (ed.), *The Symphony 1: Haydn to Dvorák; 2: Elgar to the Present Day*, Penguin Books*

SPINK, IAN, *An Historical Approach to Musical Form*, Bell

TOVEY, DONALD FRANCIS, *Essays in Musical Analysis*, Oxford University Press

ULRICH, HOMER, and PISK, PAUL A., *A History of Music and Musical Style*, Rupert Hart-Davis

* Paperback edition.

Part Four

Instruments and Voices

All art constantly aspires towards the condition of music.
– Walter Pater

The Human Voice

The oldest and most natural sound source from which music can consciously be made is the human voice. Therefore, although this chapter is primarily devoted to the discussion of the most important artificially made musical instruments used in the general concert repertoire, we shall first talk briefly about the human voice.

At the beginning of this book we saw that the essential factor in producing sound is motion which arises from a vibratory body, generating waves of compression in the air. The human voice functions on the same principle; the sound is produced by the vibration of the two tiny vocal cords which are stretched across the larynx of our throat. These cords are set into vibration by the air pumped from our lungs. The pitch of the produced sound depends on the tension of the vocal cords. The tighter the cords, the higher is the pitch of the sound, and vice versa. The sound is reinforced in the hollows of our mouth, nose, and head, which serve as resonators. The quality of the voice depends on the quality and flexibility of the cords.

The four basic categories of the human voice, which are used to describe both compass and tone-colour, are

120 The Human Voice

Bass, Tenor, Alto, and Soprano (as we have already seen in Part Two). Between them these voices encompass a range of roughly:

but both ends of it can be extended by solo singers. Here is one well-known example for each voice:

Soprano Fig. 156 (a) Mozart: 'Alleluja' from motet 'Exsultate, jubilate'

Alto Fig. 156 (b) Aria from Bach's St Matthew Passion

Tenor Fig. 157 Verdi: *Requiem*

Note that the Tenor part, when written in the treble clef, sounds an octave lower. It is thus written simply for convenience' sake. In this way fewer ledger lines are needed.

Bass Fig. 158 Aria of Sarastro from Mozart's *The Magic Flute*

We shall now look at the artificial sound-producing mechanisms called instruments. Instruments are usually classified under three main headings: stringed instruments, wind instruments, and percussion instruments.

Stringed Instruments

Stringed instruments include all the instruments in which the sound is produced by the vibration of stretched strings. These instruments are divided into three groups, according to how the vibration is set in motion: (1) *bowed* – where the string is set into vibration by the rubbing of a bow (a bow is a slightly inward-curving stick with horse-hair stretched across it); (2) *plucked* – where the vibration is made by plucking the string; (3) *hammered* – where the string is struck by a little hammer.

The Violin Family

The *violin, viola, 'cello,* and *double bass* are the most important members of the bowed-string family. They are extremely sensitive instruments, on which the most delicate nuances of tone and intensity can be reproduced.

The violin gained its final noble shape in the hands of the Amati, Stradivari, and Guarneri families. This was during the seventeenth and early eighteenth centuries: since then no important change has been made in its form.

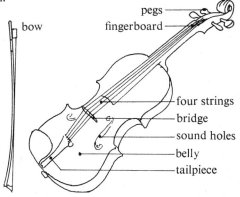

Fig. 159 The four stretched strings are tuned g, d′, a′, e″

The pitch-range
of a violin is:

The sound is usually produced by bowing the string with the *bow* while the pitches are 'stopped' with the fingers of the left hand on the *fingerboard*. This brings us to an important physical law of Pythagoras which is equally valid for other members of the violin family: *the shorter the length of a string, the higher its pitch, and vice versa.* When the string player moves his left hand on the fingerboard, he is shortening and lengthening the vibrating segment of the string.

In string parts the phrasing slur does not always indicate a unit of musical shape, but more often shows the number of notes to be played in one bow. The direction of the bowing is indicated when necessary by two signs:

⊓ = downbow; and   V = upbow.

Technical Devices of the Violin Family

Harmonics on stringed instruments can be achieved in two ways. The 'Natural' harmonic is obtained by lightly touching the open string at a certain point instead of firmly pressing it down on to the fingerboard. For example, by lightly touching the middle of any string, and bowing carefully, the note obtained will be an octave higher than the open string. In touching the string a node is produced and the string vibrates in equal segments instead of as a whole. At the node, which is the point of minimum vibration, an overtone (usually the first, second, or third above the fundamental) is reinforced. The resulting sound is clear, almost colourless in quality. When it is called for it is indicated in the parts by the use of the sign ○ above the required note (e.g. ♩).

When the normal stopping is combined with a light touch the sound obtained is called an *artificial harmonic*. The lightly touched point is always a fourth above the firmly stopped note. The result is a sound which is two octaves above the stopped note. The indication of the artificial harmonic is a white lozenge instead of a round note.

Fig. 160

Pizzicato is achieved by plucking instead of bowing the string. *Tremolo* (Italian, trembling) is indicated by putting several lines across the tail of a note (e.g.), and is the sign for the execution of very fast bowing on the same note.

Col legno (Italian, with the wood) indicates that the wood of the bow is to be used instead of the hair. *Con sordino* (Italian, with mute) indicates that the mute is to be used. This is a small clamp which is placed on or near by the bridge, so preventing the full resonance in the body of the instrument. The intensity of the sound is thus 'muted'.

Sul ponticello (Italian, on the bridge) is a direction instructing the player to bow as near the bridge as possible: the result is rather scratchy but can be apt in certain contexts, giving a somewhat mysterious effect.

Sul tasto (Italian, on the fingerboard) is just the opposite of *sul ponticello*. Here the player has to bow literally over the fingerboard. The effect is particularly mellow.

Although the stringed instruments are primarily melodic, or linear in character, it is possible to produce chords on them as well as single notes by bowing two or more strings together.

Here is an example of a typical violin solo part.

Fig. 161 Mendelssohn: Violin Concerto

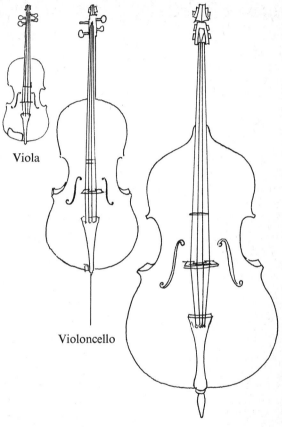

Viola

Violoncello

Fig. 162

Double Bass

The three instruments are drawn to the same scale.

The *Viola* is slightly bigger than the violin, and in comparison with it has a somewhat veiled tone.

Its four open strings are tuned c g d′ a′, and its notation is usually written in the Alto clef.

The compass of the viola is:

All the technical devices described in connexion with the violin are equally applicable to the viola, as well as to the 'cello, which is the next member of the family. Here is a fragment from one of the viola themes in Berlioz' *Harold in Italy*.

Fig. 163

etc.

The Violoncello

The *Violoncello*, or, as it is usually called, 'cello, is the bass size of the violin, and its four strings are pitched exactly an octave below those of the viola: C G d a.

The compass of a violoncello is:

Fig. 164

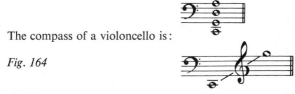

Both the violin and the viola are held on the left shoulder of the player. The 'cello, because of its size, stands on a metal *peg*, and is held between the knees of a sitting player. Its tone is very warm, like brown velvet.

Allegro moderato

mf   etc.

Fig. 165 Dvořák: 'Cello Concerto

The *Double Bass* is the lowest in voice and the largest in body of all the violin family. It also differs from the others in that it is tuned not in perfect fifths, but in fourths:

The compass of the double bass is:

Actual sounds are an octave lower.

Fig. 166

This rather heavy instrument stands on a metal peg. Because of its size the player has to stand to play it, or sit on a special high stool.

The tone of the double bass is rather dry and gruff. Technically it is far less agile than the other members of the family. Artificial harmonics are rarely produced on it because of fingering difficulties, and chords are hardly ever used, except for some two-part chords, for example A-E. It is not really a solo instrument, and is rarely used as such, but it has fundamental importance in orchestral music in that it provides a sound bass support.

Sounding an octave lower.

Fig. 167 Schubert: 'Unfinished' Symphony in B minor

Plucked instruments

The *Harp* is one of the most ancient instruments which have survived from earlier times. It has a series of strings of various lengths, which are stretched over a frame. Each string represents a fixed pitch. The strings are set into vibration by being plucked with the fingers.

The compass of the harp is C♭′ to g♭‴. This wide range is written on two staves:

Fig. 168

The modern harp is tuned to the diatonic scale of C♭. Its special technical peculiarity is that all the pitches can be chromatically altered (e.g. from C♭ to C; from C to C♯) by the use of seven pedals, which the player adjusts with his feet. Harmonics on the harp are produced by the player lightly putting the palm of one hand at the middle of a string and plucking the top part with the other. The result is a sound an octave above the normal pitch. These harmonics give a mysterious, eerie effect.

There are two special technical terms which are particularly associated with the harp, as well as with the piano. These are *arpeggio* and *glissando*.

An *arpeggio* is the playing of the notes of a chord in succession instead of simultaneously. It is indicated by

the sign ⟨ before the chord, and it is executed thus:

Fig. 169

Glissando (French *glisser*, to slide), applied to the harp, means the execution of a fast scale passage, achieved by quickly sliding the hands up and down the strings.

Here are a few bars from the harp part of Debussy's Sonata for Flute, Viola, and Harp:

Fig. 170

The *Harpsichord* is another familiar plucked instrument, the forerunner of the modern pianoforte.

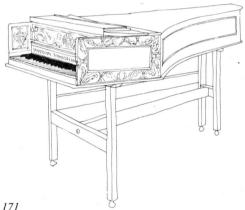

Fig. 171

The harpsichord is a keyboard instrument in which the strings are plucked by quills, or hard leathers. This is done by a mechanism which connects the keyboard and the so-called 'jack', which is a small piece of wood to which the quill is fixed. Each key has its own jack, which actually plucks the corresponding string. The usual compass of the harpsichord is five octaves, counting from F_1. Its tone is slightly dry in comparison with the piano. Nevertheless, it is an excellent accompanying instrument, and for the playing of the contrapuntal music of the baroque period to which it belongs, it is as good as, if not better than, the piano. Its part is written on two staves, like that of the harp and the piano.

Fig. 172 Bach: 'Goldberg' Variations

Hammered String Instruments

The Piano

The *Piano* (properly *pianoforte*) is a string instrument in which the strings are neither bowed nor plucked, but struck by felted hammers. The strings are stretched over a soundboard which serves to reinforce the sound. The strings are set into motion from the keyboard by a very complex mechanism which developed from the simpler mechanism of the harpsichord. The great technical improvement of the piano, in comparison with the harpsichord, is the possibility of increasing or diminishing the intensity of sound by using a heavier or lighter touch. This gives the player opportunity to produce various kinds of dynamic changes which were not available on the harpsichord (hence its name: *piano-forte*, soft-loud). Thus a closer 'personal' contact was possible between the player and his instrument.

Important mechanical devices of the piano are the dampers, and the pedals. *Dampers* are small felted pieces of wood which, the moment the key is released, automatically stop the vibration of the strings.

A piano is equipped with two pedals: the *damper* pedal and the *soft* pedal. These are both placed under the keyboard within easy reach of the player's feet. The damper pedal, when depressed, rises and lifts all the

Fig. 173

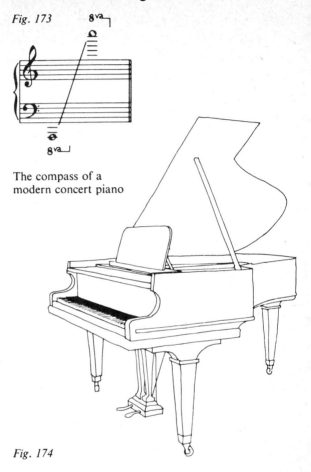

The compass of a
modern concert piano

Fig. 174

dampers away from the strings. The result is that the strings are left to vibrate after the keys have been released. The soft pedal, when depressed, moves the keyboard and the hammers a little, so that the strings are only partially hammered. The effect is a softer, somewhat muted tone.

The notation of piano music, like that of the harpsichord and the harp, is written on two staves.

Equal Temperament

We have to speak here about a matter which has particular importance in tuning keyboard instruments as
well as fundamental significance in our musical system as
a whole.

The truth is that our musical system is based on an
acoustical cheat. Correctly calculated intervals, that is,
intervals derived from the 'natural' fifth and third,
produce a disturbing acoustic phenomenon: certain
notes do not meet enharmonically. For example, B♯
actually works out *higher* in pitch than C natural.
In order to get over this intervallic difference arising from
the 'natural' calculation, instrument-builders hit on the
idea of slightly altering the pitch of all intervals except
the octave. This resulted in the division of the octave into
twelve *equal* semitones. In this way certain notes become
enharmonically equal (e.g. B♯ equals C natural). This
method simplified the construction of keyboard instruments: instead of having two keys for B♯ and C natural,
for example, one became sufficient. Above all it made
possible a richly modulatory key system. The 'circle of
fifths' discussed in Part One is based on this calculation.

Thus intervals in the tempered system, with the sole
exception of the octave, are really slightly out of tune.
This is why the piano tuner has been called the man who
is paid for making pianos out of tune. For musical convenience a compromise has been made between science
and art.

A triumphant vindication of the tempered system was
made by Bach, who in his set of Forty-Eight Preludes and
Fugues with the title *The Well-Tempered Clavier* provided
a prelude and fugue for each of the keys, major and minor.
On earlier keyboard instruments playing in 'remote' keys
would have been very tricky. But the new system was not
generally adopted in Europe until well into the nineteenth
century.

Wind Instruments

So far we have been talking about instruments in which
sound is produced by the vibration of strings, either

bowed, plucked, or hammered. In this section we shall discuss instruments in which the sound is produced by the vibration of air in a tube.

The air is set into vibration either directly by the player or indirectly by a bellows (as in the organ). The pitch of the sound produced depends on the length of the tube: 'the shorter the tube, the higher the pitch'.

Wind instruments are usually divided into two main classes – *wood* and *brass*. This distinction is somewhat misleading, because a modern 'wood-wind' instrument is not necessarily made of wood, or a 'brass' one of brass. The distinction therefore refers not so much to the material the instruments are made of, but to the way they produce sound, and also to their tone quality.

Wood-wind instruments

Flute

The modern flute is made in the shape of a cylindrical tube, usually of silver, with a parabolic 'head' at one end. It is held in a horizontal position.

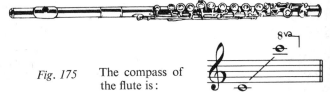

Fig. 175   The compass of the flute is:

In the 'head' end there is a mouth-hole (*embouchure*) across which the player blows air into the tube. The required sounds are controlled by covering and uncovering the holes on the body of the flute. In doing this the player shortens and lengthens the vibrating length of the tube, thus producing different pitches. Short columns of air produce high notes and long columns low notes. It is an extremely agile instrument, with a rich and pure tone.

The *Piccolo*, or 'little flute', is about half the length of a flute, and pitched an octave above it. It has a very bright sound. In order to avoid ledger lines its notation is written an octave lower than its actual sound.

Here are two familiar tunes for the flute and the piccolo.

Fig. 176 (a) Debussy: 'Prélude à l'après-midi d'un faune'

(b) Rossini: 'Semiramide' Overture

Reed Instruments

Several musical instruments use a 'sound-producing agent' made from a small, thin piece of reed, which is fixed at one end to the mouthpiece of the instrument, while the other end freely vibrates as the air enters into the tube, setting up vibration in the air column inside the tube. Some of these instruments have two reeds, vibrating one against the other. Thus we distinguish between single- and double-reed instruments.

Oboe

The oboe is a double-reed instrument made from wood, in the shape of a conical tube. The tone of the oboe is rather nasal, somewhat pastoral in character.

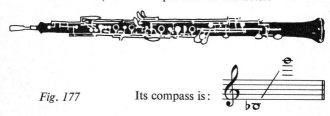

Fig. 177   Its compass is:

Here is a familiar tune from Tchaikovsky's F minor Symphony, in which the solo oboe displays its plaintive tone:

Andantino in modo di canzone

Fig. 178

Transposing Instruments

Before going further we must deal with an important
technical problem, that of the transposing instruments.
We have already encountered the fact that some instruments sound an octave higher or lower than their parts
are written (e.g. the piccolo and the double bass). But
this does not give rise to particular difficulty, because in
these cases the *key* does not change. But there are quite a
few wind instruments for which not only the pitch, but
also the key, and therefore the notation of the part, is
altered. This is done for practical reasons, and for the
convenience of the player. It has been found that in
making some wind instruments (e.g. the clarinet, horn,
trumpet) there are certain sizes which give the best results
in terms of sound and timbre, as well as making things
easier for the player. For example, the most convenient
keys for the clarinet are B♭ and A, and so clarinets are
usually made in either one key or the other. They both
require the same fingering technique, which means that a
clarinettist is able to play both clarinets with equal
facility.

Here we come to the problem of transposition: the
notation of the parts for these instruments is at a different
pitch from the actual *sound* they produce. The player
reads his music in the key which is the most convenient
for him and his instrument, regardless of the actual key
of the composition, but the sound automatically works
out at the right pitch by means of transposition. For
example, a scale in B♭ major played on a B♭ clarinet is
written out in C major but *sounds* in B♭, a whole tone
below the notation. This is particularly useful in a composition in which the key signature involves many sharps

or flats. The player of a transposing instrument has *fewer* accidentals in his part. For him there is no transposition problem: he simply plays what is written. Difficulty only arises on the part of the conductor or any reader of the music as a whole. He has to know and remember which instruments are to be transposed, and by how much, in order to play the music on the piano, and/or to hear mentally the real pitch of the instruments. This is not at all easy, and involves long and hard practice. The reader may find it helpful to note that as on the piano the simplest key is C major (i.e. it has no accidentals) so on a transposing instrument the simplest key is always the key in which it is pitched. Therefore in order to find out, for example, by how much a trumpet in E♭ has to be transposed, one simply has to find the difference between E♭ and C, and the answer is a minor third. By this method the transposition of even a rare transposing instrument can always be calculated. The pitch may work out an octave higher than necessary, but at least the key will be right, and further experience will soon eliminate this inaccuracy.

Cor Anglais

The *Cor Anglais* (English horn) is really an alto oboe, and it is pitched a fifth lower than the oboe. It is our first transposing instrument. Its part is written a fifth higher than its real sound, as shown in Fig. 179.

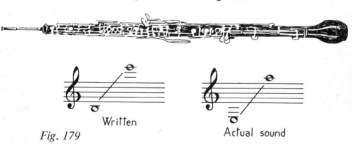

Written   Actual sound

Fig. 179

Like the oboe, the cor anglais is a double-reed instrument but with a pear-like end. Its tone is fuller than the oboe's, and expressive of a somewhat melancholic, if not tragic character.

Fig. 180 Dvořák: 'New World' Symphony

Clarinet

The *Clarinet*, as opposed to the instruments of the oboe family, is a *single-reed* instrument, made from wood or ebonite. Its pipe is cylindrical. Technically it is one of the most agile wind instruments, having a wide compass on which quick passages, arpeggios, dynamic changes, etc., can be executed very effectively.

Fig. 181

The clarinet is a transposing instrument. Nowadays the most commonly used clarinets are the B♭ and A clarinets. The notation of the B♭ clarinet is a tone higher than its actual sound, and that of the A clarinet, a minor third higher. The compass of these two clarinets is:

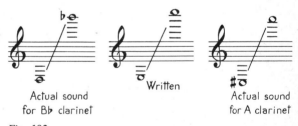

Actual sound Written Actual sound
for B♭ clarinet   for A clarinet

Fig. 182

The tone of the clarinet is rich in variety. One of its most characteristic timbres is in the so-called *chalumeau* register (after the name of a medieval wind instrument), which is the lowest octave of its compass. The notes played within this octave have a peculiarly dark tone. The upper registers are clear and very expressive; the clarinet is often called the violin of the wood-wind instruments.

Fig. 183 Brahms: Clarinet Quintet in B minor

The *Bass Clarinet*, which has a very warm tone, is pitched in B♭ and sounds a major ninth lower than its written notation.

Bassoon

The *Bassoon* is a double-reed instrument with a conical tube. The tube is a lengthy one, and in order to make it easier to handle it is bent back in two.

Fig. 184

The compass of the bassoon is:

It is the ' 'cello' of the wood-wind family, with a rich, deep tone, especially in its lower register. One of its often exploited characteristics is its undoubtedly humorous quality when used in certain ways. It could almost be called the clown of the orchestra; but like all true clowns, it can sometimes be sadder than anyone. It is a non-transposing instrument (i.e. it sounds as written). Note however that the lower octaves are written in the bass clef and the higher ones in the tenor clef.

Fig. 185 Tchaikovsky: 'Pathétique' Symphony

The *Double Bassoon*, which is the wood-wind equivalent of the Double Bass, sounds an octave lower than its part is written.

Brass Instruments

Horn

The horn (often called 'French' or 'Valve' horn) is a brass instrument with a long conical tube, which is wound round and ends in a large bell shape. Its mouthpiece is funnel-shaped. The technical peculiarity of the horn, and of brass instruments in general, is that the sound production is controlled by the player's lips, which serve as a double reed when the player presses them into the mouthpiece.

Originally the horn player was only able to produce a limited number of notes on his instrument, simply by varying his lip pressure and breathing. But with the ingenious invention of the valve-mechanism in the nineteenth century this limitation was brought to an end. The length of the air column in the horn is now made variable by the use of valves: a mechanism which, at the player's will, opens or closes the air circulation in the added pieces of tubing (or *crooks*) which are inserted into the main tube. Horns usually have three valves – controlling three additional crooks of different lengths – which enable the player to produce an almost complete chromatic scale.

The horn is a transposing instrument now normally pitched in F; this means that the actual sound is a fifth lower than its notation, which is written in both bass and treble clefs. Its compass is:

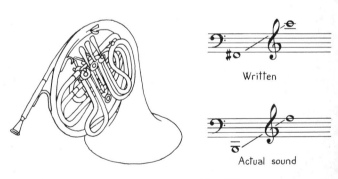

Written

Actual sound

Fig. 186   Fig. 187

and the actual sounds are a fifth lower. When pitched in C the horn sounds an *octave* lower.

By using various technical devices, such as 'stopping', 'muting', and the so-called 'cuivré', special tone effects can be produced on the horn. *Stopping* is usually indicated by the sign + over the note, and is produced by inserting the hand into the bell. The tube is thus shortened, and the sound rises a semitone, gaining a somewhat muffled quality. We have already encountered *muting* in connexion with stringed instruments. In the case of the horn the effect is similar: a veiled sound. A horn is muted by putting a pear-shaped object made of wood into the bell. *Cuivré* is the call for a harsh, 'brassy' sound, which can be produced by extra tension of the player's lips, not only when the instrument is open, but also when it is muted, or 'stopped'.

The tone of the horn is very expressive; it is capable of gentle tone, but can also produce very harsh effects. Here is an outstanding example, written for four horns. (Remember to transpose down a fifth.)

Horns in F

Fig. 188 Richard Strauss: 'Don Juan'

Trumpet

The trumpet can be thought of as the 'soprano' of the brass instruments. Unlike the horn, its tube is cylindrical, apart from its last quarter, and it has a cup-shaped mouthpiece. The story of the technical development of the trumpet is very similar to that of the horn. Originally its sound production was limited to the overtone series of its fundamental note, but with the adoption of the valve mechanism, it became a chromatic instrument. The trumpet has three valves.

The trumpet is usually pitched in C, B♭, or A. When it is in C no transposition is needed, but in the case of the

Bb and A trumpet the transposition is the same as for clarinets. Its compass is:

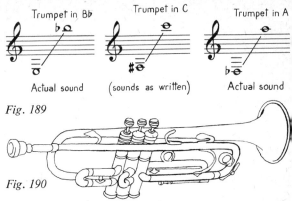

Fig. 189

Fig. 190

The trumpet has a very penetrating voice, which can easily turn to vulgarity. Technically, except in the case of very fast passages where obviously breathing problems arise, it is an agile instrument.

Fig. 191 Beethoven: Leonora Overture

The Trombones

The trombone has a unique place among orchestral instruments in that it appeared in its present shape as early as the fifteenth century (when it was called the sackbut). From that time no important technical alteration has been necessary. It has a cylindrical bore, which ends in a bell shape. Its mouthpiece is cup-shaped. The required notes are produced by moving the *slide* backwards and forwards: this is really the second part of the instrument, which slides into the first part at the player's will, so lengthening and shortening the tube. The method of playing is thus comparable to that of the violin; in both cases the players have to 'feel' the right place for the notes by ear.

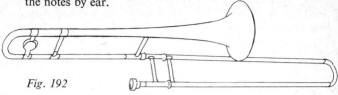

Fig. 192

The most commonly used trombones are the tenor and bass trombones. These are non-transposing instruments, the tenor trombone being pitched in B♭ and the bass trombone in G. Their compasses are:

Tenor Trombone

Bass Trombone

Fig. 193

The tone of the trombone is powerful, and somewhat similar to that of the trumpet from which it evolved, though of course the bass trombone is much fuller and stronger in its lower register. Solo parts are rarely written for trombones; they usually appear in a small group. Their notation is usually in the bass clef.

Fig. 194 Wagner: 'Tannhäuser' Overture

Tuba

Among the brass instruments the tuba possesses the lowest voice. It combines the conical bore and valves of the horn with the cup-shaped mouthpiece of the trumpet and trombone. It has four or five valves, which enable it

to produce a complete chromatic scale. The most frequently used tuba is the bass tuba. It is a non-transposing
instrument pitched in F.

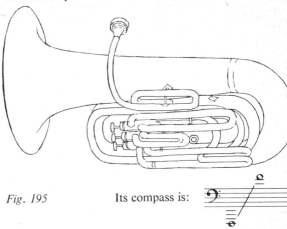

Fig. 195   Its compass is:

It is rarely used as a solo instrument, but is often heard
in combination with others, in order to reinforce the bass
line.

Fig. 196 Mussorgsky-Ravel: Pictures from an Exhibition

Percussion Instruments

The striking and the shaking of various materials in order
to create a kind of rhythmic sound is probably the most
ancient and spontaneous way of making instrumental
music. The term 'percussion' applies to all those instruments which produce sound by being either directly
struck or shaken by the player. From this very large

family the most familiar and commonly used instruments are: the Timpani; the Side Drum; the Bass Drum; the Cymbals; the Triangle; and the Tambourine. Percussion instruments can be divided into two categories: those which produce a note of definite pitch, and those which do not.

Timpani

The timpani (or kettledrums) are percussion instruments of definite pitch, consisting of a basin-shaped 'kettle', or shell, usually made of copper, across which the 'head', a sheet of calf-skin, is stretched. The skin is held by a metal ring which is adjustable with screws. The player is able to change the tension of the skin, and therefore its pitch, by tightening or loosening the screws. In modern timpani this can be done by pedals, which also make *glissandi* possible. The sound is produced by striking the 'head' with a pair of sticks which have wooden handles and felted heads.

Kettledrums are seldom used alone; there are usually two or more of them, a smaller one for the higher bass notes and a larger one for the lower.

The compass of a pair of timpani is:

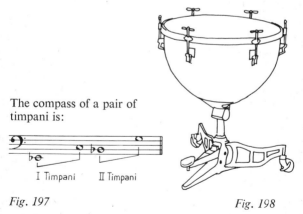

I Timpani   II Timpani

Fig. 197   *Fig. 198*

The required pitch is written in the bass clef. A familiar effect produced on the timpani is the 'roll' or tremolo, which is simply a fast reiteration of the same note. This is indicated by the sign tr〰〰〰〰 above the notes.

Bass Drum

The bass drum is a large drum of indefinite low pitch. The sound is produced by striking the stretched skin with a large soft-headed stick. Its part, which is restricted to the notation of the required rhythm, is written in the bass clef on the note C.

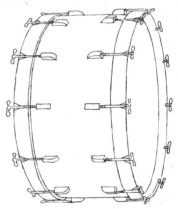

Fig. 199

Side Drum

The side drum is a small drum of indefinite pitch, with two heads tightly stretched over a metal shell. The lower head has strings of catgut (called snares) stretched across it, which give the instrument its characteristic rattling sound. These can be removed. The player strikes the top head with two sticks made from hard wood.

Fig. 200

An extremely fast roll is possible on the side drum, because of the tightness of the head, which makes the player's sticks rebound. The part of the side drum, which is purely rhythmic, is usually written in the treble clef on the note C.

145 Percussion Instruments

Tambourine

The tambourine is a small drum with one head, and with small metal plates (jingles) loosely inserted around the shell.

Fig. 201

The player either hits or shakes it with his hand. In both cases the metal plates give a jingling effect. Its part is either written in the treble clef on the g′ line, or is indicated on a single line, thus:

Fig. 202   Tambourine

Cymbals

The cymbals are perhaps the greatest 'noise-makers' of all the percussion instruments. They are two slightly concave circular brass plates. At the centre each has a handle made of leather.

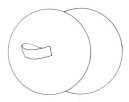

Fig. 203

The sound, which is of indefinite pitch, is usually produced by clashing one against the other. But sometimes only one cymbal is made to sound, by hitting it with one or two sticks. Its part is normally written in the bass clef. There are two technical terms to remember in connexion with the cymbals: 'laisser vibrer', indicating that the cymbals should be left to vibrate until the sound dies away; and 'sec', which means that the sound is to be cut off by damping.

Triangle

The triangle, as its name suggests, is a cylindrical steel bar bent into a triangle shape. The sound is produced by striking it with a beater also made of steel.

Fig. 204

The sound, which is of indefinite pitch, is extremely clear, in fact so bright that it can be heard even over a full orchestra playing *ff.* Its part is either written in the treble clef or on a single line, as for the tambourine.

Readers who are interested in the historical development of instruments and who would like to know more about the many other instruments (particularly percussion) which are sometimes used in the modern orchestra, can follow up the subject in the books suggested opposite. To complete this part, on pages 148–9 is a diagram showing the most usual arrangement of full choir and symphony orchestra.

Note that the plan of an orchestra often changes according to the wish of the conductor. The one given here is the most common.

The numbers of instruments in an orchestra vary greatly, but a full symphony orchestra usually has about thirty violins, which are divided into two groups (First and Second), about ten violas, ten 'cellos, and four to eight double basses. The wood-wind instruments are mostly in pairs, thus: two flutes (with one piccolo), two oboes (with one cor anglais), two clarinets, and two bassoons. The brass normally consists of two trumpets, two to four horns, three trombones, and one tuba. To these the percussion instruments are added as required.

Suggestions for further reading

BAINES, ANTHONY (ed.), *Musical Instruments Through the Ages*, Penguin Books*

BERLIOZ-STRAUSS, *Treatise on Instrumentation*, Kalmus

CARSE, ADAM, *The History of Orchestration*, Dover*

DONINGTON, ROBERT, *The Instruments of Music*, Methuen (University Paperbacks)*

FORSYTH, CECIL, *Orchestration*, Macmillan

HOWES, FRANK, *Guide to Orchestral Music*, Fontana*

JACOB, GORDON, *Orchestral Technique*, Oxford University Press; *The Elements of Orchestration*, Herbert Jenkins

MARCUSE, SYBIL, *Musical Instruments: a Comprehensive Dictionary*, Country Life

PALMER, KING, *Teach Yourself Orchestration*, English Universities Press

PARROT, IAN, *Method in Orchestration*, Dobson

PISTON, WALTER, *Orchestration*, Norton

SACHS, CURT, *The History of Musical Instruments*, Norton

WAGNER, JOSEPH, *Orchestration (a practical handbook)*, McGraw-Hill

* Paperback edition.

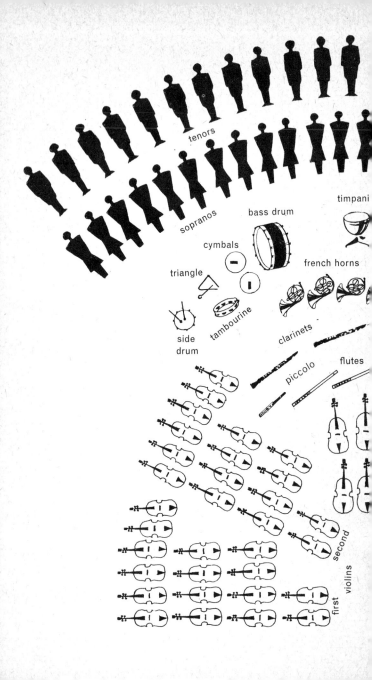

tenors

sopranos

bass drum

timpani

cymbals

triangle

french horns

side drum

tambourine

clarinets

piccolo

flutes

second

violins

first

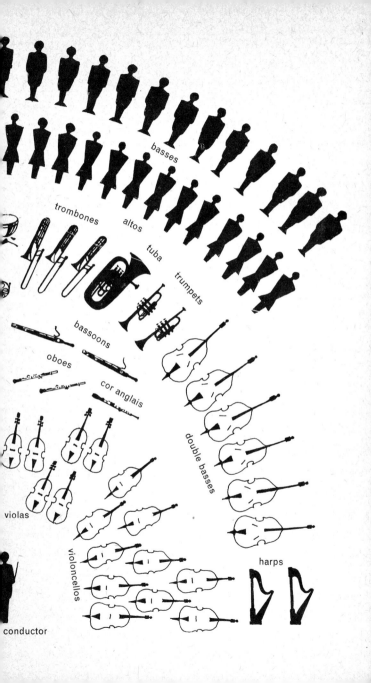

basses

trombones altos

tuba

trumpets

bassoons

oboes

cor anglais

double basses

violas

violoncellos

harps

conductor

the second time

the third ti

Part Five

Scores and Score-reading

Music, whatever sound and structure it may assume, remains meaningless noise unless it touches a receiving mind. – Hindemith

The term 'score' is generally taken to mean the written presentation of the music played by an ensemble (vocal, chamber or orchestral), arranged in such a way that its reader is able to see all the parts, and so the music as a whole, as opposed to the player who is primarily pre-occupied with his own part. As a simple illustration of this, here are the first five bars from each part of Mozart's String Trio in E♭, K.563:

Violin

Viola

'Cello

Fig. 206

152 Score-reading

In the score the parts are placed underneath each other, on different staves, thus enabling the reader to follow the music as a whole. Here now is the *score* of this Trio.

Fig. 207

The same principle holds good for all kinds of scores, small and large.

How, then, does one *read* a score? First of all, we must make a clear distinction between the *reading* and the *playing* of a score. Score-reading is being able to get the essential idea of the music written for an ensemble, that is *to hear the music mentally*. Score-playing involves, in addition, the ability to reproduce it on the piano. This requires considerable technical facility which not even all musicians possess, and the acquiring of it would break the enthusiasm of someone who does not play the piano at all. Therefore in this chapter we shall consider score-*reading* rather than score-*playing*.

Score-reading

The most important requirement in approaching a score is a consciously developed aural imagination, and this can be acquired by anyone who is not tone-deaf. Granted, the acquiring of it is not easy, and will not come simply by reading books. The ability to read a score must be the result of long practice and active musical experience. But the pleasure of intelligently grasping what is going on in a score is so rewarding that any effort made in this direction is worth while.

It is perhaps unnecessary to stress that the process of score-reading is not like reading a novel or a short story. If one can compare the two kinds of reading at all, it is possibly more like the reading of a play in verse – with careful attention to all the stage directions. If one has already seen and heard a play one can automatically recall when reading it the action, the décor, the colours of the costumes, and so on, with the same vividness as if it were actually played on the stage. Something of this kind happens with a practised score-reader.

A sound knowledge of music and familiarity with its general technique is very important. The more familiar one is with the style, idiom, and technique of various composers the easier it is to *recall* the music mentally from the score. In fact more than half the 'mystery' of score-reading consists simply in possessing a well-developed *aural imagination* and *musical memory*, which does not only mean remembering tunes, but also remembering and hearing mentally various chords, timbres, and intensities as well. Someone who is a lover of Beethoven's Fifth Symphony, and who of course is able to read music, in seeing this example:

Fig. 208

will *recognize* the characteristic motive of the first movement and will also mentally *hear* (or remember) its orchestral effect. With this elementary aptitude the hope of score-reading is granted.

Horizontal and Vertical Approaches

The recognition of the main melodies, or in other words, the *linear approach* to a score, is fairly easy to grasp and can give a would-be score-reader his first satisfaction. If you have been able to follow the examples in this book you will find little difficulty in recognizing the melody in a 'classical' score. You can often see straight away which instruments have the main tune: the strings, being the backbone of the orchestra, are certain to play it sooner or later (it is often first played by the violins), and it can be traced through the other instruments as it appears.

The recognition of motives, tunes, and various melodic and rhythmic figures is of course very important, but equally important is the recognition and hearing of the harmony. Let us take two examples, one instrumental and one vocal, and examine the harmonic functions of the chords. First, the opening of Haydn's C major Quartet, Op. 76, no. 3:

Fig. 209

Second, Handel's famous chorus from the *Messiah*:

Fig. 210

To sum up the points so far discussed, we can say that the necessary requirements in score-reading are: thorough theoretical knowledge; a trained ear which enables one to hear mentally the written music; and familiarity with the general idiom of a composer and his period.

Here someone may ask 'But what about the reading of a score one is completely unfamiliar with?' The answer is simple: in this case one has to study the score bar by bar, with extra attention, and read each part separately until the aural image emerges.

So far our examples of scores have been comparatively simple, based on the combination of three or four parts. We shall now see how the same principle works on a larger scale, as in an orchestral score where a large body of instruments is involved.

A familiar orchestral ensemble is the string orchestra, in which the instruments are: first violins, second violins, violas, 'cellos, and double basses. As an example here are the opening four bars from Mozart's Serenade *Eine Kleine Nachtmusik*.

Fig. 211

This fanfare-like opening theme does not present any problems: the only thing to remember is that the double bass sounds an octave lower than its part is written. Readers will find that the part of the double bass is often written on the 'cello staves for reasons of space. This is

always indicated at the beginning of the score thus:
Violoncello e Contrabasso.

We saw in Part Four that instruments are grouped into
four basic categories, and that in an orchestra they all
have their own place and characteristic function. Obviously this has to be clearly indicated in a score. The
accepted order of the various instruments in a score,
starting from the top, is: wood-wind, brass, percussion,
strings.

As an example of an orchestral score, here are the
opening bars of Mozart's Jupiter Symphony.

Fig. 212

Here it is easy to pick out the main tune, since most of
the instruments are playing in unison for the first two
bars. Then the first violins clearly take the leading role.

We shall now look at a few bars from the slow movement of this symphony, and try to find out what is going
on both melodically and harmonically.

Fig. 213

The movement is in *F major*, and its time signature is $\frac{3}{4}$. The tempo indication is *Andante cantabile*. There are *horns in F*, which need to be transposed to a *fifth below* their written parts, and we also have to remember that the double bass sounds an *octave lower* than written. The strings are *muted*. The opening melody is played *piano* by the first violins; at the third beat of the bar the rest of the string group enters and gives harmonic support to the melody (tonic, dominant); at the second beat of the second bar the wind instruments add to the colour and weight of the *forte*. The chord here is V⁷c in F major. At bar three the first violin group again leads with the melody, this time starting a tone higher, and at the third beat of the bar the rest of the strings enter again, but now with a new harmony (V⁷d – Ib). As in the second bar, the *forte* in bar four is played by the full orchestra. The chord here is Ib.

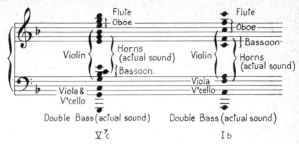

Fig. 214

If we examine the two chords played by the full orchestra as they would be written out on the piano staves, as in the example above, we notice three things: (1) the compass of the instrumental arrangement is spaced widely over the keyboard; (2) the various instruments, especially the wind, are 'blended', or dovetailed together into a homogeneous and balanced unity; (3) the various notes of the basic chord are multiplied by the instruments, so that these two chords,

Fig. 215

arranged for an orchestral *tutti*, look like Fig. 214.

The last point has a particular significance for the score-reader. It shows that an orchestral arrangement of a chord often looks more complicated than it really is; a calm approach in reading a score can make easily understandable something that first looked a mess of notes.

The next example shows the first few bars of Schumann's Piano Concerto in A minor. The place for the soloist's part is always directly above the strings. After the opening dominant note the piano leads off with a dramatic flourish; then the oboe states the theme, supported by clarinets, bassoons, and horns, the harmony ending with a cadential $^6_4$, V. The piano repeats the theme, closing with a tonic chord.

Fig. 216 (See Appendix Three for names of instruments)

Fig. 216 (Continued)

Fig. 216 (Continued)

Finally, here is a short fragment from the last movement of Beethoven's Ninth Symphony, where a choir joins the full orchestra. It is left to speak for itself.

Fig. 217

Suggestions for further reading

HUNT, REGINALD, *Transposition for Music Students*, Oxford University Press

JACOB, GORDON, *How to Read a Score*, Boosey and Hawkes*

LANG, C. S., *Score Reading Exercises in Three and Four Parts*, Books 1 and 2, Novello*

MORRIS, R. O., and FERGUSON, HOWARD, *Preparatory Exercises in Score Reading*, Oxford University Press*

RIEMANN, HUGO, *Introduction to Playing from Score*, Augener

TAYLOR, ERIC, *An Introduction to Score Playing; Playing from an Orchestral Score*, Oxford University Press

* Paperback edition.

Figuration

The reader may have noted that in some of the musical examples the melodies were derived from a chord (or vice versa). That is, the notes of a chord were used not simultaneously, but in succession, giving a melodic line (for example see Figs. 83, 141). This was, and still is, a very common unifying procedure in music. A similar, but more simple and obvious technical device is the chordal figuration which was very much in favour in the melodic accompaniment of the classical period. Here is the C major triad in some of its commonest figurations:

This stereotyped broken-chord method, when used in the bass, is usually referred to as 'Alberti bass', after the eighteenth-century Italian composer, Domenico Alberti, who was addicted to it.

Appendix Two

Tonic Sol-Fa (Solfeggio, Solfège)

The tonic sol-fa is a system of syllabic names used for sight-singing and ear-training. The principle of the system is that each note of the scale is given an easily singable syllable. Thus c d e f g a b c become do re mi fa sol la ti do. (The syllables are sometimes given slightly different spellings, e.g. doh, ray, etc.) The great advantage of this method is that it facilitates the process of learning to sight-read, since with the 'movable do' system the syllables, and therefore the corresponding intervals, remain the same in any key; i.e., do–sol will represent a fifth whether it is thought of in C major (C–G) or in C♯ major (C♯–G♯). Thus by using sol-fa it is as easy to sing in C major as in, say, F♯ major: the *do* in each case will denote the tonic of the scale. Similarly the *la* will always denote the tonic of any minor scale. Hence the English name of the system: *Tonic* Sol-Fa.

The originator of the idea was Guido d'Arezzo (see

p. 16). He used the first syllables of the Latin hymn *Ut queant laxis* as a mnemonic for the scale:

Ut que-ant la - xis re-so-na-re fi - bris Mi - - ra ge- - sto-rum fa-mu-li tu - o - rum Sol - - ve po-llu-ti la-bi-i re - a-tum San-cte Jo-an-nes

★ *Quoted from 'The New Oxford History of Music' II p. 291*

Ut later became do, and later still the leading notes ti in major keys and si in minor keys were added. Another development was the indication of sharpening by using di, ri, and fi, and flattening by using lo, ma, ra, and ta. The following examples illustrate how the method works.

a) Bach: Two part invention in C major

do re mi fa re mi do sol do ti do

b) transposed to C♯ major

do re mi fa re mi do sol do ti do

a) Bach: Three part invention in F minor

la do ti ti re di re si la_sol fa mi re do

b) transposed to A minor

la do ti ti re di re si la_sol fa mi re do

Foreign Names of the Instruments

The names of the instruments are sometimes given in a score in German, Italian, or French. The following list gives the foreign names of all the instruments discussed in Part Four, in the order in which they appear in a score.

English	German	Italian	French
Piccolo	*Kleine Flöte*	*Flauto Piccolo (Ottavino)*	*Petite Flûte*
Flute	*Flöte*	*Flauto*	*Flûte*
Oboe	*Hoboe*	*Oboe*	*Hautbois*
Cor Anglais	*Englisches Horn*	*Corno Inglese*	*Cor Anglais*
Clarinet	*Klarinette*	*Clarinetto*	*Clarinette*
Bass Clarinet	*Bassklarinette*	*Clarinetto Basso (Clarone)*	*Clarinette basse*
Bassoon	*Fagott*	*Fagotto*	*Basson*
Double Bassoon	*Kontrafagott*	*Contrafagotto*	*Contre-Basson*
Horn	*Horn*	*Corno*	*Cor*
Trumpet	*Trompete*	*Tromba*	*Trompette*
Trombone	*Posaune*	*Trombone*	*Trombone*
Tuba	*Tuba*	*Tuba*	*Tuba*
Timpani	*Pauken*	*Timpani*	*Timbales*
Triangle	*Triangel*	*Triangolo*	*Triangle*
Tambourine	*Schellentrommel*	*Tamburino*	*Tambour de Basque*
Cymbals	*Becken*	*Piatti*	*Cymbales*
Bass Drum	*Grosse Trommel*	*Gran Cassa (Tamburo)*	*Grosse Caisse*
Side-drum	*Kleine Trommel*	*Tamburo militare*	*Tambour militaire*
Harp	*Harfe*	*Arpa*	*Harpe*
Violin	*Violine*	*Violino*	*Violon*
Viola	*Bratsche*	*Viola*	*Alto*
Violoncello	*Violoncell*	*Violoncello*	*Violoncelle*
Double Bass	*Kontrabass*	*Contrabasso*	*Contrebasse*

American Usage

American and English usage of musical terms have diverged in a few details. The most important of these, in the order in which they appear in this book, are as follows:

English		*American*
note (meaning sound of definite pitch, as distinct from 'noise')		tone
semibreve	○	whole-note
minim	♩	half-note
crotchet	♩	quarter-note
quaver	♪	eighth-note
semiquaver	♬	sixteenth-note
demisemiquaver	♬	thirty-second-note
hemidemisemiquaver	♬	sixty-fourth-note
bar		measure
time		meter

168 Index of Signs

ξ	crotchet rest	ρ̄	tenuto
⅞	quaver rest	‖o‖	breve
⅞	semiquaver rest	o	semibreve
⅞	demisemiquaver rest	♩	minim
⅞	hemidemisemiquaver rest	♩	crotchet
	breve rest	♪	quaver
	semibreve rest	♪	semiquaver
	minim rest	♪	demisemiquaver
	bar-line	♪	hemidemisemiquaver
	double bar-line	c′	middle C
2/4	time signature		staff *or* stave
	repeat sign		ledger lines
𝄴 4/4	('common time')	𝄞	G clef
𝄵 2/2	*alla breve*	𝄢	F clef
♩.	dotted note	𝄡	C clef
⌒	tie or slur	{	brace
⌢	pause sign		
ρ̂	sforzando		play an octave higher
ρ̇	staccato		play an octave lower
ρ̌	staccatissimo	*fff ff f mf* *mp p pp ppp*	dynamic marks

⟨crescendo sign⟩	crescendo	♯	sharp
⟨decrescendo sign⟩	decrescendo	♭	flat
⟨triplet notation⟩	triplet	$\left.\begin{array}{c}\sharp\sharp\\\times\end{array}\right\}$	double-sharp
⟨quintuplet notation⟩	quintuplet	♭♭	double-flat
⟨appoggiatura notation⟩	appoggiatura	♮	natural
⟨acciaccatura notation⟩	acciaccatura	I	tonic
⟨upper mordent sign⟩	upper mordent	II	supertonic
⟨lower mordent sign⟩	lower mordent	III	mediant
⟨turn sign⟩	turn	IV	subdominant
$tr\sim\sim$	trill	V	dominant
⟨key-signature notation⟩	key-signature	VI	submediant
		VII	leading note
IIb, etc.	first inversion	⊓	down bow
Ic, etc.	second inversion	V	up bow
V⁷	dominant seventh	⟨natural harmonic sign⟩	natural harmonic
II⁷, etc.	secondary seventh	⟨artificial harmonic sign⟩	artificial harmonic
V⁹	dominant ninth	⟨tremolo notation⟩	tremolo
V¹¹	dominant eleventh	⟨arpeggio sign⟩	arpeggio
V¹³	dominant thirteenth	+	stopping
N⁶	Neapolitan sixth	⟨figured bass notation⟩	figured bass
A⁶	augmented sixth		

General Index

174 General Index